A GLOSSARY

OF

SPANISH BIRD-NAMES

A GLOSSARY
OF
SPANISH BIRD-NAMES

KEITH WHINNOM

TAMESIS BOOKS LIMITED
LONDON

Colección Támesis

SERIE A - MONOGRAFIAS, III

Depósito Legal: 12.338 - 1966

Printed in Spain by Talleres Gráficos de EDICIONES CASTILLA, S. A.
Maestro Alonso, 23 - Madrid

for

TAMESIS BOOKS LIMITED
LONDON

This book is published with the aid of a subvention from the University of the West Indies.

CONTENTS

ACKNOWLEDGEMENTS

I am grateful to Mr Brian Dutton, hispanist and ornithologist, of Birk-beck College, London, in conversation with whom the idea of this Glo-ssary was conceived and whose criticism of an early draft was most help-ful; to Dr Dafydd Evans, expert on French and Provençal bird-names, of Queen Mary College, London, for his comments and observations; to Dr Ivan M. Goodbody, Professor of Zoology, U.W.I., who looked for ornithological errors; to my colleague Mr W. Mailer, whose search for ambiguities clarified several obscure statements; to Professors M. F. M. Meiklejohn of Glasgow and P. E. Russell of Oxford, who made various valuable suggestions; and to my secretary, Mrs Stella Mitchell, for her careful and patient typing of an exacting manuscript.

INTRODUCTION

The present work is not an attempt to treat Spanish bird-names historically (though it has consequences for etymologists); it does not pretend to be (though one would hope that it comes close to being) an exhaustive repertory of Peninsular Spanish bird-names; and it is far from being the final answer to the problems of the lexicographers (though it should save future dictionaries from some of the grosser errors). All that I have tried to do here is to collect in one place, from a variety of sources, the names which appear to attach to distinct species of birds, to codify this evidence, and, occasionally, to offer some comment on its validity. It is probable, indeed, that such value as this work may possess lies in the questions it poses and the doubts it casts on accepted identifications, rather than in the answers it provides.

In a methodological essay on bilingual lexicography Edwin B. Williams wrote: «Given the name of an animal or plant in one language there is no surer course to the name in the other language than the Latin name of the genus and species.» [1] The precept is ultimately, and in principle, unarguable, but matters are not nearly so simple as Williams's statement might lead one to believe. In the first place there does not exist a satisfactory Spanish list of the type required, and the lexicographer who attempts to follow this prescription will encounter manifold difficulties of other kinds which have no easy solution. The present glossary is an attempt to remedy in part the major deficiency, while in this introductory essay I endeavour to describe the kind of problems which, though I confine my remarks to bird-names, are to be met with in the translation of vernacular zoological nomenclature in general.

Basic problems

It is possible to draw a line across Europe (taking in Northern France) dividing—somewhat crudely—north from south, German from Latin, Protestant from Catholic, and, simultaneously, languages and dialects with complete repertories of popular names for birds, plants, fishes, and so on, from languages lacking complete inventories of names. How far back one can trace this difference of attitude to Nature—certainly it antedates

[1] 'The problems of bilingual lexicography, particularly as applied to Spanish and English', *Hispanic Review* XXVII (1959), 246-253, p. 247.

the Industrial Revolution, but it is not so readily demonstrable that it antedates the seventeenth-century scientific revolution, and even less, the Reformation—and with precisely what factors one should link this interest in Nature, it is difficult to determine. But there can scarcely be any disputing the fact.

An eminent French dialectologist has suggested that peasant communities are interested only in useful (edible?) and harmful birds and plants:

> Rarement abstrait, le lexique de la langue paysanne est encore strictement utilitaire: des plantes et des animaux qui fourmillent dans les champs, le paysan ne nomme que ce qu'il connaît de toute évidence comme utile ou nuisible; quant au reste il témoigne d'une ignorance et d'une indifférence à peu près totales. [2]

This accords, of course, with Malinowski's experiencies in Polynesia:

> In a forest, a plant or tree would strike me, but on enquiry I would be informed—'Oh, that is just «bush».' An insect or bird which plays no part in the tradition or the larder, would be dismissed 'Mauna wala'—'merely a flying animal'. But if, on the contrary, the object happened to be useful in one way or another, it would be named. [3]

But while it would be possible to describe the Spanish situation in similar terms, I do not accept the conclusions that might be implied: that industrialization and urbanization lead to the repair of these deficiencies *in the dialect terminology,* or, possibly more important, that this ignorance or indifference is the rule in all peasant communities. The Swedish peasant, who knows his birds, is not more industrialized than the Italian; nor are the Shetland fisher-folk, who distinguish by name every diver, duck, tern, and gull, more scientifically-minded than the Spanish fishermen who call all gulls *«gaviotas»*. Why these differences should exist is not readily explicable (I lean towards the notion that the Spanish situation is the norm, and the other a peculiarly Germanic phenomenon), but exist they do. Anyone who has had experience of trying to discover Spanish bird-names will have an anecdote to parallel D. H. Lawrence's «È un fiore».

In various European countries, Germanic and Latin, difficulties of another kind have stemmed from the absence of a nationally accepted inventory of bird-names. The standardization of names is a phenomenon

[2] P. Nauton, *Le patois de Saugues* (Clermont-Ferrand 1948), p. 41. I owe this reference to Dr Dafydd Evans with whom I have in correspondence disputed the thesis that the situation in Britain is due to the early onset of industrialization and hence of a more widespread scientific outlook.

[3] Bronislaw Malinowski, Appendix: 'The problem of meaning in primitive languages', to C. K. Ogden and I. A. Richards, *The Meaning of Meaning* (New York 1944).

to be connected directly, on the purely linguistic level, with the encroachment of a standard language on the dialect areas, and, no doubt, more broadly, with the spread of books and such phenomena as industrialization and the diffusion of a scientific outlook. In France a *Commission pour l'unification des noms français des oiseaux* was set up in 1933, and the *Inventaire* published in 1936 by Mayaud makes considerable use of names drawn from different dialects as bases for a binomial system, e.g. *Hibou grand-duc*; [4] and similar problems of establishing a standard system of nomenclature have presented themselves, and been similarly solved, in Germany, [5] and, very much more recently, in Spain. But the situation with regard to English names is quite different. It is, indeed, unique in the world.

English bird-names

In England there has been a continuous tradition of ornithological studies at least from the seventeenth century. If William Turner, in the sixteenth, like other Renaissance humanist ornithologists, adds little to the information supplied by Pliny and Aristotle, [6] towards the end of the following century the monumental work of Willughby and Ray is already on a scale grander than anything yet written by a Spaniard, and Ray can open his preface to the English edition with an apology for producing yet another book on birds—«after so many books on this subject already published» (f. A2). [7] There are a score of major works, running to two, three, eight, even ten volumes, before 1800; [8] and then the avalanche begins. To check the classified index of a copyright library is an impressive experience: [9] literally thousands of books on birds have been published in Britain, and they are still pouring out, now at an average rate of *one every two weeks*. These facts have an important bearing on the lexicographer's problems.

The curious English interest in «Natural History» has meant, to remain within the ornithological field, that not only the birds of the

[4] Dr Dafydd Evans. For further information on the problems of standardization of French names see Mayaud in *Alauda,* 1934, pp. 114-115, and H. Jouard, *ibid.,* 1933, pp. 500-510.

[5] See B. Hoffmann, 'Verhandlungen der ornithologischen Gesellschaft', *Bayern* 18, pp. 318-336.

[6] William Turner, *Avium praecipuarum, quarum apud Plinium et Aristotelem mentio est, breuis et succincta historia* (Cologne 1544), reprinted with introduction, translation, notes, and appendices by A. H. Evans as *Turner on Birds* (Cambridge 1903). Turner lists 132 species, supplying English names for 112.

[7] The original in Latin by Willughby, *Ornithologiae libri tres: in quibus aves omnes hactenus cognitae ... decribuntur ... totum opus recognovit, digressit, supplevit J. Raius* (London 1676) was published in John Ray's translation, with his emendations and amplifications, as *The Ornithology of Francis Willughby* (London 1678).

[8] A bibliography of the more lavishly produced items, by Buchanan, may be found in Sacheverell Sitwell, H. Buchanan, and James Fisher, *Fine Bird-books 1700-1900* (London and New York 1953).

[9] The privilege of the library of Trinity College, Dublin, dates from 1801.

British Isles but virtually every bird in the world, of all 30,000 species, has been equipped with an English name (though not always, of course, any more «English» than «kangaroo»—cf. «jacana», «hoatzin», etc.). The standard studies of the birds of North and South America, Australia, Africa, South-east Asia, India, the Middle East, are all in English; and for the Palaearctic region the only rival language is German. The book-names established and propagated by this vast literature are unequivocal and remarkably stable, and I suspect that those unacquainted with the work of Willughby and Ray might be astounded to see how many clearly non-popular terms, such as «Lesser spotted woodpecker», have remained standard since the seventeenth century.

There is certainly, even among the book-names, a multiplicity of synonyms, arising from distinct sources, but they are now almost entirely obsolete, and the only remaining problem of any importance is the reconciliation of American with British English for the species held in common. The stability of the English book-names was affected, mainly in the nineteenth century, in various ways. Some ornithologists tried to impose names which they felt to be more fitting: so that, for instance, the non-specific element [10] of a complex name, like «sparrow», «wren», or «plover», might be abandoned when the bird in question was shown to be unrelated to the sparrows, wrens, or plovers; or an eccentric might make an effort to popularize «Brown-headed gull» on the grounds that the black of the Black-headed gull's head is not really black. In addition many unwieldy names, invented for newly discovered and described birds, were simplified; while, from another direction, the stability of the book-names was threatened by those writers on British birds who tried to give wider currency to dialectal, popular, names, liking their savour and authenticity, and wishing to avoid the colourless pattern of adjective-(adjective)-non-specific. But the standard pattern of English book-nomenclature (Lesser, Black-, White-, Red-/spotted, backed, tailed, headed/woodpecker, gull, eagle, bunting) has inestimable advantages, in that, given an adequate basic repertory of non-specifics, it may be extended to cover an almost infinite number of exotics, such as «Violet-eared dove», «Rough-winged swallow», or «Arrow-headed warbler». [11] And the book-names have now almost entirely replaced the local names, even in the spoken language. But—and this is the other extraordinary point about English bird-names—the obsolescent dialect-systems which the standardized system of book-names has replaced reflect the same interest in natural objects and were also complete systems: repertories of names

[10] I use the term «non-specific» for a name which indicates, not a single species, but a group perceived or believed to be «related»: «eagle», «goose», etc. I reserve «generic» for «pertaining to a scientific genus». In English terminology, words may be at once specific and non-specific, and in ornithological literature are distinguished by the initial capital of the specific (cf. Redstart/redstart), a well-worn convention which I also observe here, to the extent of using *one* initial capital for a complex name. Technical usage requires capitals for qualifier *and* non-specific element.

[11] Not my inventions, they are, respectively, *Zenaida auriculata, Stelgidopteryx ruficollis,* and *Dendroica pharetra.* See James Bond, *Birds of the West Indies* (London 1960).

for all the locally-occurring species have been recorded for almost every area. [12]

In short, English bird-names are fairly stable, and almost completely unequivocal. From any one of several thousand sources the lexicographer can produce an English name, if not invariably «the» English name, for any bird occurring in the British Isles, and, from a wide variety of other sources, names for foreign birds. At every point this situation contrasts with Spain and Spanish.

Spanish names (i): ornithological works

Leaving aside the medieval manuals of hawking [12 A] and the Renaissance translations of and commentaries on Aristotle and Pliny, there have been published very few Spanish books about birds—hardly, until very recently indeed, more than a dozen in all. When Spanish ornithological writing (in the serious scientific sense) began, in the nineteenth century, authors had neither a book-tradition to follow nor—and I return to this point—a complete popular repertory of names. They were in general obliged to refer to their birds by means of the scientific Latin.

[12] Bibliography may be found in H. Kirke Swann, A Dictionary of English and Folk-names of British Birds (London 1913). I find that this work contains all and more than the material in similar and earlier compilations, such as those of C. Swainson, The Folk-lore and Provincial Names of British Birds (London 1886), Charles Louis Hett, A Glossary of Popular, Local, and Old-fashioned Names of British Birds (London 1902), or H. E. Strickland's uncompleted Ornithological Synonyms (London 1855). The vast majority of Swann's 5,000 synonyms are folk-names, now obsolete, completely replaced by the book-names.

[12 A] Although I have chosen to avoid the historical treatment of bird-names, it would scarcely be justifiable to pass over the medieval literature on falconry without any comment. All the medieval manuals give detailed and careful accounts of every aspect of their subject; but it is extremely difficult to extract from them the kind of information I have aimed at providing. In the first place, their attention is focussed exclusively on the art of hawking (of the value of which in the training of warriors all writers have inflated notions), to the extent that all birds tend to be classified quite simply into the birds of prey which can be trained for the chase, the birds they can profitably be flown at, and—a tacit third category—the remainder, which are of no interest whatsoever. It is surprising to discover how few bird-names these works contain: Juan Manuel, Libro de la caza, ed. J. M. Castro y Calvo (Barcelona 1947) mentions only 37, of which 13 are birds of prey, and the remainder, except for the «rosinor», their quarry, while Pero López de Ayala, Libro de la caza de las aves, ed. J. Gutiérrez de la Vega (Madrid 1879) mentions 12 birds of prey and 10 others. Furthermore, while some treatises, like Ayala's, appear at first sight to supply precise and detailed descriptions of the hawks (but never of their quarry), the purpose of these descriptions is not recognition, and identification is not always a simple matter. As Castro y Calvo puts it (ed. cit., p. 173): «Un problema al parecer fácil, pero que entraña alguna dificultad, es [la] identificación de los pájaros de presa citados en los libros clásicos»; and one finds that the editors and commentators of these texts offer conflicting and sometimes disconcerting interpretations which it would take too much space to list and comment on here. I should like to suggest, however, that the key to the difficulties which editors have encountered lies in the difference between medieval and modern conceptions of species. The medieval falconers distinguished Gyr, Greenland, and Iceland falcons, Peregrine, Mediterranean, and

5

One early writer [13] noted a few popular Andaluz names, while two of the most important writers of the century attempted to create a set of book-names. [14] But their endeavours must be reckoned almost a total failure, partly because there was no volume of subsequent literature to reinforce them, but largely because the systems are themselves inadequate and unsystematic. They use strange inventions based on the scientific Latin: *plectrófano de las nieves*<*Plectrophenax nivalis, locustela fluvial*<*Locustella fluviatilis, erismaturo leucocéfalo*<*Erismatura leucocephala,* etc., or simply use the Latin itself where it can be taken into Spanish without modification: *clángula histriónica, fuligula marila,* etc. Ventura de los Reyes, knowing no Spanish names for certain birds, notes down the Catalan. Popular Spanish names of indefinite connotation (*churrica, mosquitero,* etc.) are arbitrarily attached to birds quite rare in Spain, while there are, finally, great gaps in the system: birds for which no Spanish name is supplied at all. Other details might be mentioned, but it is hardly necessary to insist on these curiosities. I have noted these names in the present glossary (J^1, see p. 32) but clearly little authority attaches to them, and, needless to say, few of these coinages have found their way into Spanish dictionaries, although some do occur in some of the older and larger bilingual dictionaries.

I have not attempted to explore thoroughly, though I have looked at some of, a number of rather marginal works, many published in the nineteenth century, on hunting and shooting, agriculture, and natural history in general, which do supply some bird-names. The information they provide is often given obliquely: that is, as in the medieval treatises on hawking, the authors tend to assume that a bird is sufficiently clearly identified by its very name, so that, for instance, a work on agriculture will say that among useful, insectivorous, birds which should not be killed are ... and there follow various popular names; with regard to the books on shooting, it may be noted that the game-birds are the one category of birds about which there is least confusion; and the general works on natural history appear to provide no information that is not covered by the more specialized ornithological works. The authors of

Barbary falcons; by attempting to match, name for name, the medieval catalogue of hawks and falcons against a modern scientific checklist of species—and forgetting the subspecies—editors have frequently found themselves with four falcons too few, and have proceeded to fit to medieval names birds which one doubts were ever used in falconry at all, like the Lesser kestrel and the Buzzard. However, Bertil Maler's edition of the *Tratado de las enfermedades de las aves de caza* (Stockholm 1957) clearly demonstrates that the whole medieval literature of falconry, Latin, Spanish, Portuguese, Provençal, French, Italian, and German—and one should probably add English and Arabic—is interdependent to an extraordinary degree, so that a full-scale examination of all the available texts may eventually clear up all the difficulties.

[13] Antonio Machado, *Catálogo de las aves observadas en algunas provincias de Andalucía* (Seville 1854). I have ignored him in this glossary on the strength of Lord Lilford's remarks (L, see p. 33) about him. Machado labelled the ornithological specimens in the Seville museum—erroneously, according to Lilford.

[14] Ventura de los Reyes y Prosper, *Catálogo de las aves de España, Portugal e Islas Baleares* (Madrid 1886), and José Arévalo y Baca, *Aves de España* (Madrid 1887).

the new *Diccionario histórico de la lengua española,* of which I have more to say later, are currently engaged in the labour of extracting bird-names (among other things) from this literature.

In complete contrast with the earlier ornithologists is Augusto Gil Lletget (Ll, see p. 33), who makes no attempt to invent names, but records, sporadically, genuine «nombres populares». This is, of course, incidental to his purpose, which is not linguistic, and from the linguistic point of view the work leaves much to be desired. Only just over half the birds are given Spanish names at all (203 out of 391); Catalan names, and what from other sources I have discovered to be Galician (the phonology does not always make it apparent), are mixed indiscriminately with Castilian, and no note is made of the regional currency of the various terms; certain names recur for a variety of birds (*almendrita, azulejo,* etc.); many well-known bird-words are not to be found here at all; and, probably most serious of all, the book is badly misprinted. A *fe de erratas* lists eighteen mis-spellings (in one instance emending an acceptable Spanish «espátula» to an unacceptable «spátula»)—or approximately a fiftieth part of the misprints the book contains (I count 880 in 215 pages). One cannot, therefore, after having to emend *carabo, neblín, pedreo,* etc., to *cárabo, neblí, pedrero,* etc., accept even the spelling of some of the more unusual names with confidence. This is all the more unfortunate in that Lletget is the sole authority for some very interesting bird-words not recorded in any of the standard Spanish dictionaries.

I have found nothing else of note in Spanish ornithological writings before the recent creation, in 1955, of a complete standard system of Spanish nomenclature. The foundation of the *Sociedad Española de Ornitología* in 1954, and the publication by its secretary, D. Francisco Bernís, of a check-list of Spanish birds, in the first issue of the first Spanish ornithological journal, *Ardeola* (B[1], see p. 32), means that Spanish writers on birds, who may be expected to become increasingly numerous, will now employ these «official names» to the exclusion of others. A century or two hence, lexicographers will scarcely need to look further afield.

Throughout the *lista patrón* Bernís has been extremely ingenious. Except for a few of the most distinctive birds, which retain their popular one-word name, he has endeavoured, while using singularly few coined words, to establish a binomial system (trinomial for subspecies) which goes hand in hand with the scientific Latin. So, for example, we have *ánade silbón* and *ánade friso,* not just *silbón* and *friso,* the popular names, for the Wigeon and the Gadwall. As a consequence, popular ambiguities are avoided: Marbled teal and Partridge, both *pardilla,* are clearly distinguished as *cerceta pardilla* and *perdiz pardilla.* Regional or learned synonyms are distributed, so that the various words for «warbler» label the various genera: *buscarla* for birds of the genus *Locustella, carricero* for *Acrocephalus, zarcero* for *Hippolais, curruca* for *Sylvia,* etc. He

7

has, in short, brought order into chaos and labelled unambiguously every Spanish bird. Furthermore, as with English book-names, the system is easily extended on the same pattern, and almost anyone can do it. Thus *Gavia adamsii,* the White-billed diver (American «Yellow-billed»), which does not figure on the Spanish list, would clearly be *colimbo de Adams, colimbo piquiblanco,* or *colimbo piquigualdo.* The generic name is established by Bernís, and the qualifier is almost invariably a rendering of the scientific Latin or the English qualifier. It requires only an authority to fix the form it shall take. González Díez (B², see p. 32), with Bernís's advice, in fact opts for *colimbo de Adams.* Difficulties arise only with genera not represented on the Spanish list, and González Díez meets them by adapting the scientific Latin (cf. *parula americana, niotilta varia,* etc.), a procedure more easily defensible for the exotic strays for which no Spanish names exist than for more common birds.

Bernís's is a noteworthy achievement. But his system is arbitrary, in the sense that the vast majority of the terms in the *lista patrón* are «Spanish» only in so far as a Spaniard sat down and thought them up. The system has also one grave disadvantage in being so closely tied to the scientific Latin. Anomalies are already apparent in this glossary, particularly among the passerines, where I have followed the revised taxonomy of Vaurie (see p. 22). The scientific Latin nomenclature is chronically and necessarily unstable, reflecting as it does continuous progress in knowledge. Two species are lumped into one, a species is split into two or assigned to a different genus, so that Bernís's system is already partially in decay. His generic terms are in the process of becoming merely non-specifics, while «splitting» and «lumping» wreck his binomial-trinomial system (cf. Glossary Part I, Nos 362 and 363, split; Nos 381, 381a, lumped).

There are a few other very minor points open to criticism: etymological errors like *andarríos de Terek* (for *del Terek:* the Terek river defined as the type-locality by Güldenstädt in 1775), inadequate distinctions like *pinzón común/pinzón vulgar,* and the complete ignoring of American Spanish popular names. This latter point is quite important. It is absurd to label the ubiquitous Spur-winged plover of the Argentine pampas «*avefría espolada*» when it is universally known in South America as the *tero* (with variants *terutero, teruteru, terotero*). Many of the American birds which find their way into the European list by virtue of one or two storm-blown casuals are equipped by González Díez with exotic labels although they are to be found in Mexico and the Caribbean and have popular Spanish names.

However, the principal defect of the system from the lexicographer's point of view—and it is no criticism of the system as such—is that it is the creation of one man: it does not represent popular Spanish usage. It has also had the rather unfortunate side-effect of putting an end to the recording of popular names in the ornithological literature. Thus Guy Mountfort, writing about larks in Spain in 1954 (M, see p. 33),

8

supplied large numbers of popular and regional names; but his book on the Coto Doñana expedition carries an appendix of Spanish bird-names confined exclusively to the official check-list.[15] (On the Catalanization of the official Spanish nomenclature I shall have something to say later.)

Spanish names (ii): encyclopaedias and dictionaries

Only one Spanish encyclopaedia need detain us, the remarkable *Enciclopedia Espasa-Calpe* (E, see p. 32). The *Enciclopedia* is ornithologically sound, since it derives its information from the standard authorities in English, German, and French (cf. the items listed in the bibliography s. v. *ave:* twelve German, eleven English, five French, one Dutch, *no* Spanish; or s. v. *abejaruco,* where it even quotes Dresser's *Monograph on the Meropidae),* but its handling of names is subject to no coherent policy. The scientific Latin terminology is not only far too frequently misprinted (misprints constitute a very real problem in many of the sources with which I have had to deal), but is used quite inconsistently, so that the same bird may appear in different volumes under several different Latin disguises (depending on the date of the source of the information) without anything to warn the unwary that the Latin terms are synonymous; while the English names, which are occasionally supplied and could have provided a firm point of reference, are often unacceptable («owlet», etc.). This means that it sometimes requires some effort to discover which bird is under discussion, and a few bird-words, without any Latin names, would remain, without evidence from other sources, completely mysterious *(alionín, pájaro trapaza, trullo,* etc.). As for «Spanish» names, the situation is completely chaotic. In the earlier volumes the scientific Latin names used as main entries or titles of illustrations are consistently hispanicized: *cocotraustes (coccothraustes) quetusia (Chettusia), carádridas (Charadriidae),* etc., etc., and one is left in grave doubt whether the authors are proposing the adoption of the Latin as Spanish. Very often no vernacular names are supplied at all, so that, for example, s. v. *ánade, Anas acuta, A. penelope,* and *A. strepera,* all ducks by no means uncommon in Spain, are never mentioned by their Spanish names. S. v. *pato,* there is an incomprehensible insistence on Chilean names, so that of thirty-two vernacular names listed, twenty are Chilean («nombre chileno», «nombre que en el sur de Chile se da...», «es la que se encuentra en Chile», etc.), and there is an equally curious abundance of names from Álava throughout the work. Catalan names intrude everywhere, sometimes Castilianized, like *margaso* (Cat. *margassò)* sometimes in a weird half-way house like *pasera de las rojes* (Cat. *pàssera de les roges),* sometimes unequivocally Catalan. S. v. *oología,* the vernacular name of *Pyrrhocorax graculus* is given as *gralha de pico vermelho* (doubly

---

[15] *Portrait of a Wilderness: the Story of the Ornithological Expeditions to the Coto Doñana* (London 1958). Similarly, *El mundo de las aves: enciclopedia ilustrada* by Jean Dorst, translated by Montserrat Andreu and R. S. Torroella (Barcelona 1963) uses only the «official» names for European birds.

in error). There is no coordination between the earlier and later articles, so that vernacular names mentioned under one heading are differently employed elsewhere, while cross-references frequently lead nowhere. S. v. *alionín* one is referred to *paro,* whence one is referred to *párido,* where there is no mention of *alionín;* under *halcón coronado* one reads «V. ARPELLA», but there is no such entry; *camachuelo* says «V. PARDILLO», but under *pardillo* the word *camachuelo* does not appear. Some of the Spanish vernacular names which are supplied have no support from other sources (see Glossary Part I), and other Spanish names are defined only as American birds, though other evidence shows us that the name is current in Spain for a European bird. The Espasa-Calpe encyclopaedia is the source of confusion which is reflected in serious errors in, among others, Corominas's *DCELC* and Gili y Gaya's *Vox* dictionary.

Nevertheless, despite all its numerous and grave faults, and the lack of a coherent system of nomenclature (which accurately reflects the state of affairs in Spain when it was published), the *Enciclopedia* does supply a very large number of Spanish names which, treated with due caution, may be of value. But it is necessary to insist that no «Spanish name» supplied by E can be accepted as authoritative without confirmation from a genuinely independent source. [16]

One may also attempt to pursue bird-names in Spanish dictionaries. I have used three (not exhaustively) in this Glossary: the Academy's, as the standard authority, Miguel Toro's *Pequeño Larousse ilustrado,* an unusually independent work, where identification of the birds is often assisted by the little pictures, and Gili y Gaya's *Vox* dictionary which, alone among general Spanish dictionaries, makes use of the scientific Latin (with somewhat unequal success) to identify the various terms. [17]

There are a great many criticisms to be levelled at the Academy's definitions of bird-names. Perhaps the most important is that the Academy makes no use of the Latin nomenclature (though it usually does so for plants) and offers quite undistinctive descriptions: there are too many «smallish brownish» birds which might each be any one of a score of different species. In the entries for the owl-words, once we are told that we have to do with an «ave de presa nocturna» (which is not always accurate) the major part of each description is irrelevant and unnecessary, detailing the hooked beak, the forward-facing eyes, the soft plumage and noiseless flight, the talons, etc. «Cuántas veces», as Menéndez Pidal exclaims, «echamos de menos indicaciones diferenciadoras en la definición de plantas y de aves». [18] But distinctive differences are perhaps the

---

[16]   The reader who attempts to check in E itself the names cited with its authority in Part I of the Glossary may encounter some difficulty. A very large number of these terms are not listed in their alphabetical position in the encyclopaedia but are given under a hispanicized Latin entry or under such headings as *oología, pájaro, fauna de España,* etc. It would have been impossible to indicate the precise context without greatly increasing the bulk of this monograph.

[17]   Of the *Duden español,* Corominas, Martín Alonso, and the new *DHLE* I have something to say later.

[18]   Prologue to V (see p. 33), p. xxi.

10

province of the expert, and the fact is that the Academicians are clearly victims of their own innocence in a totally unfamiliar world. A48, for instance (it is corrected in 56), tells us that *according to popular superstition* («según opinión común») the cuckoo lays its eggs in the nests of other birds (s. v. *cuclillo*). Or again, A48 carefully describes a *corneja* in quite unmistakable terms as a Hooded crow, although this bird is only a very rare visitor to Spain. One might have supposed that even the Academy could have described a crow with fair success.... In contrast with the vague and undistinctive descriptions, we find, occasionally, painstakingly detailed descriptions of purely mythical creatures: one or more details must be wrong, the habitat, the size, the colour—of beak, head, neck, back, breast, or legs—but one does not know which item to emend. Consider, for instance, the Academy's *trullo:* a minimum of three emendations must be made in the description given to identify it with any known species, and as it stands it defies identification. [19] Finally one must mention the Academy's insistence on defining non-specifics as specifics. Words like *somorgujo* or *petrel* indicate whole families of birds; but the Academy carefully describes a species in each case, for *somorgujo* what appears to be the Black-necked grebe, for *petrel* what might be either the Storm-petrel or Wilson's petrel—an «indicación diferenciadora» is lacking. In short, even when the Academy's dictionary offers an unequivocal description for any given bird-name it is possible that it is wrong, and one cannot accept it as authoritative. Descriptions in the *Pequeño Larousse* are even less detailed, though, as I have said, the illustrations occasionally assist one to identify the bird intended. Miguel de Toro would also appear to be, at times, the victim of the confusion existing in the French-Spanish bilingual dictionaries.

Gili y Gaya's *Vox* dictionary is a good deal more helpful than the Academy's, making use as it does of the scientific Latin nomenclature. However, the principal source of Gili y Gaya's ornithological information is quite clearly E, and though the Catalanisms and similar peculiarities of E are not carried over into V, the unidentified bird-words (*buharro, trullo,* etc.) remain unidentified in V, and the disorganized scientific Latin synonymy of E leads to even greater chaos in V. So, for instance, *pico verde* is labelled *Gecinus viridis,* while, with a different description, *pájaro carpintero* is identified as *Picus viridis Sharpei:* but the Latin names are synonymous. The Spanish description sometimes does not match the Latin name, as, for example, *cuchareta:* «ave zancuda de América, de pico en forma de espátula (*Spatula clypeata*)»; the description indicates the

[19] *Trullo* is something of a mystery. The consensus of opinion among the bilingual dictionaries is that it means «Teal», and Mr Brian Dutton informs me that it is used in León for the Teal and related species. But the Academy's description (of which Gili y Gaya's is a drastically reduced summary) in eight out of nine characteristics does not match *Anas crecca.* Corominas (s. v. *trulla* II) refers to a further strange detail: «el nombre aludirá al buche prominente a modo de pelícano». E says only that it is an «ave del orden de las palmípedas parecida a la cerceta», while P, even less helpfully, defines it as a «género de aves palmípedas que pasan el invierno en España».

Spoonbill—though it is a Spanish bird too—but the Latin name is that of a duck, the Shoveler. *Grigallo* is described as being a little larger than a Partridge (and seems to be the Black grouse), but it is identified as *Tetrao urogallus,* the Capercaillie, which is enormously larger. *Doradillo,* if it means a wagtail at all, must be *Motacilla flava* and not *Motacilla alba.* And so on—I cite only some illustrative cases. Finally one finds here lists of Spanish synonyms—most useful in principle—which other sources suggest are by no means always synonymous.

I have scarcely used Corominas's *DCELC* (except for the following section) simply because the vast majority of his bird-names, defined only as «cierto pájaro», are unidentifiable. Martín Alonso's *Enciclopedia del idioma* has neither detailed descriptions nor scientific Latin, and I have employed it only to construct the «Appendix of names not recorded in Spanish dictionaries». There are several technical dictionaries, not all of which I was able to see, which include bird-names, but those I did see I discarded on discovering that the information, including the antique and misprinted scientific Latin, appeared to derive from E, and that they were in any case less complete than V. There remains the new *Diccionario histórico de la lengua española,* which has not yet progressed far enough to be of much help. It uses scientific Latin, but does not get off to a too promising start, in that one of its very first bird-words, *abanto,* appears to be wrong. [20]

Finally, I have incorporated all the bird-names from what is really a bilingual dictionary, the *Duden Español* (D, see p. 32). While the colour-plates are unequivocal, and the black and white sketches are executed with care, this «pictorial dictionary» would present a series of enigmas if it were not for the supplementary English index (or the *English Duden),* since it would be quite impossible, with no clue as to size or colour, to tell, for example, that 346-17 is a Thrush-nightingale, or 346-8 a Siskin. It is clear that most of the names in D derive from E, not only because of the sustained coincidence of the terminology, but also because of the repetition of some very peculiar terms, like *chimbo de cola roja* and *gargolet.* Nevertheless D also has various names which do not appear to depend on E, and some fourteen which I have not found recorded in any other source. Again, while the list is, obviously, very

[20] It is identified as *Vultur monachus* (i.e. *Aegypius monachus,* the Black vulture), with the observation that «en algunas regiones de España se da o se ha dado este nombre a otras especies de la misma familia, como el buitre, el alimoche, y el quebrantahuesos». But the first citation, from Alfonso X, «es aue aque llaman otra guisa quebranta huessos», should probably be interpreted, not that *avanto* is applied to the *quebrantahuesos* (Bearded vulture), but that *quebrantahuesos* is applied to *Neophron percnopterus* (which is certainly the situation today). The quotation from Martínez Espinar, 1644, «poco menor que el buitre», excludes the Black vulture (which is larger), and indicates the *alimoche.* The *Diccionario de agricultura,* 1939, supports this, while Arévalo, 1887, limits the synonymous use of *abanto* and *alimoche* to the Sierra Nevada. My information indicates that (i) *abanto* is synonymous with *alimoche* in Castile and Andalusia; (ii) it is never applied to the Black vulture; (iii) it is never applied to the Bearded vulture, though *quebrantahuesos* is applied to various birds besides *Gypaëtus barbatus.* The *DHLE* may be right, but there is a case for regarding this pronouncement with a touch of scepticism.

far from exhaustive, and while one might dispute several of the equivalences (I do not believe, for instance, that *verderón* is a Spanish name for the Yellowhammer, nor *becada* a name for the Snipe), the general impression of ornithological competence (due to its source, the *Duden Bildwörterbuch*), the refreshing lack of ambiguity (due to correct use of the English terminology), the careful distinctions made between specific and non-specific terms (by means of the definite and indefinite articles), and, perhaps not least, the impeccable printing, have persuaded me to include it in this Glossary.

It may be necessary at this point to make it absolutely clear that what may appear to be very severe censure of these dictionaries is not to be construed as a general reflection on their worth. I am concerned only with bird-names. The lexicographer cannot be an expert in all spheres of knowledge and must rely on other works of reference: the deficiencies of existing dictionaries are due entirely to the absence of the essential micro-glossaries. But it is important at this stage that the honest guess of a hard-working linguist should not, by sheer repetition, achieve the status of unassailable authority; and I hope this may serve as some kind of apology (if it is necessary) to, particularly, Gili y Gaya and Corominas.

Spanish names (iii): an excursus on owls

Accurate identification is perhaps of greatest moment to the etymologist, and it is worth digressing a while to show what the dictionaries do with the owls—and how suspect, consequently, the proposed etymologies must be. Corominas has a little essay on the subject of the European nomenclature of owls (s. v. *mochuelo* III, p. 395):

> El estudio de la nomenclatura de las aves de presa nocturnas está oscurecido por el gran número de variedades de las especies principales, variedades a veces poco distintas, y por la gran confusión que por esta razón o por falta de cuidado, reina en los diccionarios bilingües. En España las más conocidas son el buho, la lechuza y el mochuelo, y será bueno indicar sus equivalencias en los idiomas vecinos, con el objeto de aclarar las ideas y evitar equívocos. La equivalencia respectiva parece ser port. *bubo, coruja* y *noitibó,* mientras que *môcho* parece haberse aplicado a estas dos últimas aves; cat. *duc, òliba* y *mussol;* gasc. *uhoun* (o *gaüs*), *gaueco (gabeque)* y *tchut (tchout, tchot);* fr. *grand-duc* (o *grand hibou*), *chat-huant* (o *hibou moyen*) y *chouette;* it. *gufo, allocco* y *civetta;* lat. cl. *bubo, otus* (o *asio*) y *noctua;* alem. *uhu, eule* y *kauz;* en inglés todos se llaman *owl,* con calificativos, el buho es *horned-* o *eagle-owl,* la lechuza *screech-owl,* el mochuelo quizá *owlet.* Las denominaciones científicas varían mucho según los autores y las casi infinitas variedades (se cuentan hasta 200 estrígidos en total), las tres más típicas son, respectivamente, el *Bubo bubo,* la *Strix flammea* y el *Glaucidium passerinum.*

The «confusion» has proved too much even for a lexicographer as erudite and scrupulous as Corominas, who has been led seriously astray largely by the eccentricities of E (and has been, perhaps, a little frightened by the thought of there being two hundred distinct species of owl loose on this earth). «Horned owl» (or «horn-owl») is in British English a synonym (an old book-name and a still extant dialectal name) for the Long-eared owl, not the Eagle-owl, which is a very irregular visitor to England, while in American English «Horned owl» (or «Great horned owl») indicates what English ornithologists term «American eagle-owl» or «Virginian eagle-owl». (It is of the utmost importance, for bilingual lexicographers especially, to keep distinct British and American English.) But this bird is *Bubo virginianus,* not *Bubo bubo.* [21] Of course it is clear that Corominas is not really confused about the first of the three terms which he tries to clarify: a *buho* means for him an Eagle-owl *(grand-duc, grand-duc ordinaire, grand hibou, hibou grand-duc* in French, *Uhu* in German, *duc* in Catalan, *gufo* or *gufo reale* in Italian, and *bufo*—not *bubo*—in Portuguese). But the Academy at least does not agree with him, and what he intends by the other terms is less easy to determine. *Strix flammea,* now (and for many years past) *Tyto alba,* can be called «screech-owl» in English—it is the Barn-owl—but not in American English, where the Screech-owl, *Otus asio* (to English ornithologists «American screech-owl») is quite a different bird. But *Tyto alba* is not *chat-huant* in French, but *effraie* or, in the standardized terminology, *chouette effraie, chat-huant* indicating the Tawny owl, *Strix aluco.* The Italian *allocco* is also used, at least in the technical literature, for the Tawny owl, not the Barn-owl, which is *barbagianni.* The German terms are no help at all, since both *Eule* and *Kauz* mean simply, non-specifically, «owl» (cf. *Schleiereule, Zwergohreule, Waldohreule, Sperlingskauz, Wald-kauz, Steinkauz,* etc.). The Portuguese equivalents are equally baffling, since it would seem that both *coruja* and *mocho* are non-specifics. [22] Only the Catalan *òliba* indicates unequivocally the Barn-owl.

The third set of terms is perhaps even more confusing. *Glaucidium passerinum* is the scientific name of the Pygmy owl, which lives in Scandinavia, Siberia, and Eeastern Europe, and could not possibly be des-cribed in Spain as one of «las más conocidas». [23] «Kauz» and «owlet» do not really «aclarar las ideas», while «chouette» is a non-specific applied with qualifiers to the Pygmy owl, Little owl, and Barn-owl, not to mention the Hawk-owl, the Great grey owl, the Ural owl, and

[21] It has now been suggested that the two are conspecific, i.e., that they are sub-species of the same species.

[22] The situation in Portuguese is as complex, and for the same reasons, as in Spanish. I have used A. C. Smith, 'A sketch of the birds of Portugal', *Ibis* 1868, 428-460; William C. Tait, *The Birds of Portugal* (London 1924), who takes some trouble over local names; J[1]; B[2], which gives names based on W. C. Tait, systematized by Geoffrey M. Tait; and Morais's *Dicionário.* The bilingual dictionaries are even worse than the Spanish-English.

[23] Lletget's *Sinopsis* (Ll) includes it, citing no record of its occurrence, but it is rejected by the official Spanish check-list. Part of the confusion in Corominas stems from E, which, s. v. *mochuelo,* has a picture of *Glaucidium passerinum.*

Tengmalm's owl. Portuguese *noitibó* means «nightjar», [24] which is, of course, not an owl at all, and *mocho* is ambiguous as I have said. But Italian *civetta* and Catalan *mussol* indicate, without qualifiers, the Little owl, and Corominas goes on to say that *Glaucidium passerinum* is the «mochuelo común» described by the Academy under *mochuelo*—a bird 20 cms long. The dimensions (and the geographical distribution) rule out *Glaucidium passerinum* but permit of two possibilities: the Scops owl or the Little owl. Since Corominas is in process of an etymological argument to the effect that *mochuelo* means «without horns», the ear-tufts of the Scops owl leave us with only the Little owl. To Corominas therefore *buho, lechuza,* and *mochuelo* mean Eagle-owl, Barn-owl, and Little owl. But leaving aside the Gascon (of which I know nothing) and the Classical Latin (the meanings of the middle two terms appear to be anyone's guess), the only language in which he has contrived to express these facts accurately is Catalan. And although in these three cases he does appear to be right, a *cárabo* is not a *lechuza,* and an *autillo* cannot be both *cárabo* and *lechuza,* and may be neither. To get a coherent picture one needs to consider more than three species of Spanish owls.

The Academy arranges various owl-words in groups of synonyms: *alucón, cárabo, úlula, zumacaya, zumaya* = *autillo; bruja, curuca, curuja, estrige* = *lechuza; corneja* = *buharro;* while *buho, mochuelo* and *miloca* are not equated with any other terms. The descriptions supplied, though mostly redundant after «ave de presa nocturna», contain some significant details. The *lechuza,* 35 cms long, yellowish white, with a «graznido estridente» is unmistakably the Barn-owl. The *autillo,* a little larger than the *lechuza,* and reddish, can only be the Tawny owl—provided that we can assume no mention of ear-tufts means that the bird has none. The *mochuelo,* 20 cms long, with yellow eyes and no mention of ear-tufts, which «abounds in Spain» must be the Little owl. But the *buho,* 40 cms long, with ear-tufts, must be the Long-eared owl, for the Eagle-owl is a bird almost twice as large. The *buharro,* then, which is described as being like the *buho,* but smaller, and with ears, must be the Scops owl, while the *miloca,* the same size and shape as a *buho,* would seem to be the Short-eared owl. The Eagle-owl is left unaccounted for. But the Academy's illustrated dictionary does not entirely agree with the larger one. [25] The pictures of *autillo, lechuza,* and *buho* could just pass for the birds indicated by the descriptions in the larger dictionary; but the *mochuelo* is certainly not a Little owl, for it has prominent ear-tufts.

The *Pequeño Larousse* also has pictures of owls; but except for the *lechuza,* which is unmistakably a Barn-owl, the others, *autillo, buho,* and *mochuelo,* are all drawn with ears, which neither the Tawny owl (apparently the Academy's *autillo*) nor the Little owl (the Academy's *mochuelo* in the larger dictionary) possess. In fact the *Pequeño Larousse* does not

---

[24] B[2] limits it to the Nightjar, using *boa-noite* for the Red-necked nightjar. I strongly suspect that this distinction is quite arbitrary, though possibly useful to ornithologists.

[25] Real Academia Española, *Diccionario manual e ilustrado de la lengua española* (Madrid 1927).

make sense, for it also lists *buharro* and *miloca* as separate species, and describes them as being like the *buho*. We have too many eared owls here. The *Petit Larousse,* which uses the same blocks, only makes the confusion worse, and is in any event inaccurate also. [26]

Gili y Gaya's struggle with the owl-words is interesting in that his attempts to reconcile E with the dictionaries lead him into an impasse. He groups the same synonyms as the Academy for *lechuza* and identifies it by means of scientific Latin (if somewhat outmoded) as the Barn-owl; *autillo,* with the same synonyms, is the Tawny owl; *buharro* is the Scops owl; *buho* is the Eagle-owl; and *miloca* is Tengmalm's owl. But *mochuelo* is left as a minor mystery. Gili y Gaya had sorted out his owl-words quite nicely but was left with a *mochuelo* which defied placing. On the one hand there was the consensus of the dictionaries that a *mochuelo* was a distinct species—not, for instance, the same as a *buharro*—and on the other, there was a picture of a *mochuelo,* an owl with ears—the identical block to all appearances—in P and the illustrated A. Unable to discover yet another small eared owl he solved the problem by adopting A's definition: «20 cms long, eats rodents», and appears to have had his artist copy the drawing from one or other source: the bird illustrated (s. v. *rapaces)* is so outlandish that the resemblance cannot be coincidental. Necessarily he was forced to omit in this case any scientific Latin name.

If Bernís (B[1]) is not simply being arbitrary in calling the Scops owl *autillo,* the Tawny owl *cárabo,* the Little owl *mochuelo,* and using *mochuelo, lechuza, cárabo,* and *buho* as non-specifics in addition, the expert makes nonsense of the dictionaries, and some of the proposed etymologies are untenable: the Scops owl does not hoot «*a-ut*», and *mochuelo* is not reserved for earless owls. The additional evidence I have collected for this *Glossary* does not by any means finally solve these problems, revealing as it does large-scale confusion, but I hope that it brings us a little closer to a correct answer in disposing of some wrong answers.

All this is not untypical of the various dictionaries' handling of bird-names in general. Even the most conscientious lexicographers, like Gili y Gaya and Corominas, who have clearly made strenuous efforts to achieve accuracy, fall into error. It is true that things are even worse in the bilingual dictionaries, where confusion is worse confounded by inability to handle the English synonymy, and, often, failure to distinguish between American and British English, [27] but they are hardly to be blamed for the

---

[26] Claude Augé and Paul Augé, *Nouveau Petit Larousse Illustré* (Paris 1924). The pictures use the same blocks as the Spanish: *hibou* and *mochuelo* are identical, as also *chouette* and *autillo* (all with ears). This would make a *mochuelo* an Eagle-owl. The new edition of 1959, with photographs, clears up much of the confusion by defining various owl-words as non-specifics; but the same queer drawing of an *hibou* appears next to a photograph of the face of an Eagle-owl. The new Spanish edition, 1964, appeared too late for me entirely to revise the P entries, but a brief examination suggests that no radical changes would have been necessary.

[27] The one conspicuous exception is Edwin B. Williams, whose *Holt Spanish and English Dictionary* (New York 1955) represents, so far as the bird-words are concerned, a complete break from the tradition of copying from Velázquez. His

·confusion among Spanish lexicographers. The reality is not impossibly complex. There is, for instance, something less than an «infinite variety» of *Strigiformes* to contend with: Peters [28] lists only 143 for the whole world, of which only fourteen occur in Europe and only nine in Spain. But some expert knowledge is required, and the prime cause of the confusion is the lack of it. However, while it should now be abundantly clear that a dictionary-definition does not constitute a guarantee of accuracy, one may also begin to wonder whether the now «official» names used by the experts are not sometimes arbitrarily assigned and how far they are a reliable guide to the «real meaning» of Spanish bird-names.

Before leaving the Spanish sources I should say something about the numerous dialect-studies which, inevitably, include some bird-names. Those I examined almost invariably explained the dialect term by a better-known bird-word such as *lechuza, vencejo,* or *alondra,* or others of whose meaning I was even less sure. This is perhaps rather an excuse than a sound reason for ignoring them. But the fact that existing studies rarely mention more than a handful of birds, a profound mistrust of the ornithological expertise of Spanish dialectologists, the availability of other, reliable, sources, and the immensity of the task of searching for bird-names through this extensive literature, deterred me. In the long run, of course, the correct meaning of bird-names can be established only by extensive field-work done by dialectologists who are also competent ornithologists—though their task will still be bedevilled by confusion among their informants. The present Glossary is only a beginning, an attempt to make use of existing information.

Spanish names (iv): the English ornithologists

If the sources I have described were all one had to draw on, the outlook would be discouraging. However, a vast amount of work on Spanish birds has been published outside Spain, principally in England. I have seen over a hundred books and articles on the subject; and of these a good proportion record Spanish vernacular names. One can be completely confident that the bird in question is accurately identified, and that, in the sources I have used, the Spanish name represents an honest attempt to set down the name supplied by the informant. I have

---

owl-words are sorted out most competently. I hope it is not hypercritical to note (1) that the (necessarily) restricted selection of bird-words means that many, including some of the most puzzling, are omitted; (2) that it is important in using a term like «screech-owl» to indicate whether it is being employed in the American or British sense; (3) that it is legitimate to enter archaic terms in the English-Spanish section, but not to offer them as translations in the Spanish-English, e. g. «*becafigos,* fig-pecker»; and (4) that a number of the translations offered, while they may well be correct, do not agree with other authorities, so that, e.g. *tordo alirrojo* may indeed be a Song-thrush but in the view of E, A, P, and V (and more plausibly, in my view) is the Redwing.

[28] James Lee Peters, *Check-list of Birds of the World*, 6 vols, uncompleted (Cambridge Mass. 1931-48), vol. IV (1940), pp. 77-174.

ignored the many possible sources which either recorded only a handful
of names amply confirmed by other evidence or borrowed extensively
from Saunders or Irby. These sources have not, to my knowledge,
been exploited before, and they form the most important contribution
to the present Glossary. Reading them, one begins to come to grips
with the realities of the situation.

Lord Lilford (L) was one of the pioneers. In 1865 he wrote that the
birds of Spain are «less known than those of any other part of Europe
of equal extent» (p. 166). «It is very unusual to meet any Spaniard who
cares for, or occupies himself about, any branch of Natural History»
(p. 169). «I have generally found that the lower orders in Spain refer
the inquirer to the province of Estremadura for every beast or bird
concerning which they know little or nothing. 'En Estremadura hay mu-
chos', has been said to me about almost every bird in the country» (p. 170).
And, returning to the topic in 1866, «There is no work whatever on
general Spanish zoology,...I much fear that any general attention to
Natural History in Spain will long remain a thing of *mañana*» (p. 385).
He explains further that he has himself noted down only those names
which he has heard in use, and sometimes includes valuable additional
information, such as: «The Spaniards call all the large Vultures *Buitre,*
occasionally distinguishing [the Griffon] as *Buitre franciscano*»; or:
«[Bonelli's eagle] is known in Andalucia as *Perdicero* and *Aguila blanca,*
which last appellation is indeed given to many other species», etc.

Howard Saunders (S) in 1871 remarks on the Castilianized forms of
scientific names to be found in Spanish local lists and concludes that
«their admission would be of little benefit», again preferring to cite only
those Spanish names he has himself ascertained to be in common use.
In 1875 Irby (I) wrote extensively on the subject of Spanish vernacular
nomenclature. I quote, without emending the orthography or the obsolete Latin (revised ed., p. 5):

> As a proof of the inaccuracy of local nomenclature, a single name
> is often applied to several species, sometimes not even belonging
> to the same genus. Thus *Aguila, Aguilucho,* according to the
> ideas of the individual, may be any of the Diurnal Accipitres,
> from a Lammergeyer to a Lesser Kestrel; and they are even
> occasionally used to designate the Raven! !
>
> So *Bujo* applies to *all* Owls, *Culiblanco* to *all* Wheatears;
> *Chorlito,* the real name of the Golden Plover, is used for various
> Waders; while *Pitillo, Frailecillo, Andarios, Correrios,* are in-
> definite names applicable to any small Waders and some larger
> ones. *Pito real* near Gibraltar is *Picus major,* our Great Spotted
> Woodpecker; near Seville it is *Gecinus Sharpii,* the representa-
> tive of our English Green Woodpecker *(G. viridis).* *Carpin-
> tero* in Central Spain, according to Lord Lilford, is *Picus major;*
> near Gibraltar it is the Great Titmouse *(Parus major).* *Lavan-
> dera,* or «washerwoman», according to localities is either a Wag-

tail or a Green Sandpiper. *Quebrantahuesos,* «bone-breaker», properly applies to the Lammergeyer; but where that species is absent it is usurped by the *Neophron.*

These, among other instances, prove local names to be only an assistance, and not always to be taken to signify the bird to which they are affixed.

On the other hand, some names are distinctive, as *Abejaruco,* Bee-eater; *Abubilla,* Hoopoe; *Abujeta,* Godwit; *Alcaravan,* Stone-curlew, etc.

Abel Chapman and Walter Buck (C³) frequently remark on the prevailing Spanish ignorance in matters ornithological. When they finally found a man who knew what a *quebrantahuesos* was they comment (p. 298): «Francisco's ornithological reputation was easily acquired, for among the blind a one-eyed man is king.»

More recently, Captain P. W. Munn, who has supplied a list of Catalan local names, [29] wrote of the inhabitants of the Balearics: [30] they «have little knowledge of the birds or of the natural history of their district, and are not interested as a rule in natural objects; even the shepherd boys, who spend the whole day in the country with their flocks, take very little notice of the birds around them: little reliance can, therefore, be placed on their statements.» In 1954 Guy Mountfort (M, p. 111) could write: «The Spanish vernacular names quoted vary from one region to another and are sometimes applied to more than one species; it is not possible to localize them.» This latter remark is something of an exaggeration: the expression of the frustration of an ornithologist uninterested in dialectology, and accustomed elsewhere to being able to report «the vernacular name». But from this collection of plaints three facts emerge which have considerable importance: popular ignorance and indifference, the wide currency of non-specific names, and great regional variation. The absence of an established body of literature on the subject, together with the popular failure to notice any but the largest, brightest-coloured or edible birds means that many Spanish species simply do not have Spanish names, apart from the newly-invented official ones.

As a consequence, one is brought, at times, to the threshold of the problem of the meaning of meaning. If, when Lord Lilford is told that a Sparrow-hawk is called *cernícalo,* we can be fairly sure that his informant simply did not know the difference between a Kestrel and a Sparrow-hawk, [31] there are trickier cases in which usage must be allowed

---

[29] In Fred Chamberlin, *The Balearics and their Peoples* (London 1927), chap. XV, 'The Birds of Majorca and Minorca', pp. 147-173.
[30] 'Notes on the birds of Alcudia, Majorca', *Ibis* (1921), pp. 672-719.
[31] I may be wrong about this. Dr Dafydd Evans has pointed out to me that the use of *cernícalo* to designate the Sparrow-hawk is parallelled in France, where the *Falconidae* are divided into two groups, the large and the small. A non-specific, «small diurnal bird of prey», covers Sparrow-hawk and Kestrel; the name itself tends to be a kestrel-name (referring to the distinctive hovering), but this is counterbalanced in other areas by the historical importance of the Sparrow-hawk in falconry.

to sanction the «mistake». *Avión* and *vencejo,* which in the official terminology are «martin» and «swift», are apparently used interchangeably because of a popular failure to distinguish between martins and swifts. In practice both words are synonymous non-specifics used to indicate swallow-shaped birds not swallows. But there is every shade of ambiguity between what seems obvious error: «eagle» for «raven», «stork» for «heron», and so forth, and the modern confusion of terms which, not entirely because of regional variations, indicate more than one species or groups of species which one feels ought to be distinguishable, and would perhaps be distinguished in some hypothetical «correct» usage.

As Irby has pointed out there are, comparatively, very few entirely distinctive bird-names in Spanish. The vast majority of one-word names are non-specifics, and many species are not distinguished at all from related or similar birds. One can discard the evidence of the peasant who offers «Es un pájaro» (or «crío de pica» for the Pied wagtail), [32] but the fisherman who says «Es una gaviota» is doing his best: there is no other name for the vast majority of the many species of sea-gull. The group *grajo-graja-grajillo-grajilla* is used generally for all black-feathered members of the *Corvidae,* except that the diminutives exclude the Raven, and it is probably pointless to attempt to distinguish meanings within the group, And not only related species but distinct families and orders are confused in popular usage. This complicates the business of translation. Various ornithologists have insisted that English names are not strictly generic: e.g. «Strictly speaking a common name has no generic, specific or sub-specific term, but it often has the appearance of being made up of a generic and a specific term». [33] But in practice English names follow very closely scientific groupings, of genus, family or order. Popular Spanish names do not, so that on the one hand there is no Spanish word for «owl» except the paraphrase «ave rapaz/de rapiña/de presa nocturna» (which is not always accurate—there are diurnal owls) or the learned creation «estrígido», while on the other hand we have Spanish words that denote something less than a genus and cover a semantic area smaller than an English non-specific («buho», «grajilla», «herrerillo») or something greater than a scientific group and more than the English («águila», «alondra», «perdiz»). There are Spanish non-specifics, perhaps to be reckoned of another type, which may not imply recognition of any relationship at all: «azulejo», applied to various birds which have a bit of blue about them (Kingfisher, Roller, Bee-eater), «castañita», applied to various small brown birds, or «carbonero», applied to various small black or black-capped birds.

Finally there are the regional names, which, as explicitly pointed out by Irby, vary even within the broadly distinguished dialectal areas. The evidence of Verner, who records different usages between the mountains and the plain, goes to show that even within Andalusia one must

[32] I owe this nice example to Mr Brian Dutton, who met it in Castellón.
[33] R. D. MacLeod, *Key to the Names of British Birds* (London 1954), p. 3.

distinguish between province and province, between Gibraltar and Seville, between the villages of the *sierra* and the hamlets of the *marismas*.

These facts present extremely difficult problems for the bilingual lexicographer. I shall deal with the precise difficulties in the course of explaining the exact nature of the present Glossary.

The Glossary (i): its scope and range

The Glossary consists of two parts: the first a classified list of birds with the names I have been able to collect for each species, the second an alphabetical list of the Spanish names. It is supplemented by an Appendix of the names not recorded in the dictionaries, and an English index.

The birds are those known to have occurred in Europe and in Spain. «Spain» has birds not on the European list, since officially it includes the Canary Islands. In the circumstances the birds of the Spanish Sahara are perhaps arbitrarily excluded. [34] The list is thus essentially B^1 supplemented by B^2. To be precise the *Field-guide* list (B^2) does not include every bird known to have been reported in Europe; but it is impossible to draw a clear-cut line. One has to cope, not only with highly dubious reports from western Ireland in 1843, but also escaped cage-birds. Naturally the extra-peninsular birds have usually only book-names, but even here there is no hard and fast rule: the medieval falconers imported a number of birds not native to Spain which are now equipped with «Spanish» names. Sources for American Spanish I have, with the exception of Leopold (Le), ignored, though in a few obvious cases, such as that of the Spur-winged plover, Spanish dictionaries supplied the authority to note more than its invented official name. For most of the exotic strays from the New World it would have been possible to supply a number of popular American Spanish names (varying, of course, from region to region, from Mexico, to Cuba, to the Dominican Republic, to Puerto Rico); but I have not undertaken to do so.

I have made an exception in the case of Leopold's list of Mexican bird-names because we have to do here, not only with exotic casuals but with common European birds. Mexico is the one Spanish American country whose avifauna coincides to any exent with that of Spain—to a slightly lesser degree than that of the United States with that of Britain. The birds involved are, particularly, the *Anatidae,* and include such familiar creatures as Mallard and Teal, Gadwall and Shoveler.

The Glossary (ii): classification and scientific Latin

The Glossary lists 570 species of birds, including one extinct species, No. 283. Subspecies are lettered under the same figure. The scientific Latin nomenclature is chronically unstable, as I have mentioned, and, for the common European birds, probably the surest guide for the inexpert reader is the English name. The vaunted precision of the

[34] Studied in J. A. Valverde, *Aves del Sahara español* (Madrid 1957).

3

scientific Latin is indeed a snare and a delusion for anyone without access to the specialized literature which keeps track of the changes. I have not myself attempted to do so. For the non-passeres the nomenclature and classification is essentially that of B², which represents the state of knowledge in 1957. The birds in B²'s appendix of rarities, and those of the Canary Islands, have been placed in the appropriate positions on the authority of various more modern sources. For the passeres I have used Vaurie [35] who incorporates all the information available up to 1958. His is the most recent coherent reassessment of the classification of the *Passeriformes;* but I have departed from B² not simply in the interests of scientific accuracy but in order to illustrate the way in which Bernís's system begins to break down in the wake of advancing knowledge. The arrangement of species in the glossary, by genus, family, and order (from the most primitive to the most advanced), is customary ornithological procedure, but it has the further advantage for the lexicographer of grouping related types and so making it easier for him to find the vernacular generic and non-specific names.

Subspecies present various problems. Nearly all the English names for subspecies, or «races», are of fairly modern creation, and there has been, more recently, a very strong reaction against using them at all: «the desirable occasions for using them are much fewer than current practice would suggest.» [36] I have used them therefore only in three situations: where there is a distinct Spanish name for the subspecies in question and the English subspecific provides an exact translation; where the English name in current use «attaches firmly to what at present is regarded as a race» and when the «problem of finding an acceptable and unambiguous name for the species as a whole» has not been solved and appears insoluble (cf. No. 380); and finally, but only in the English index, where well-established names formerly regarded as specific (Iceland falcon, etc.) are now reckoned to be names of races. In one sense some of the American names listed in the English index might be regarded as subspecific names, for Duck-hawk obviously must refer to *Falco peregrinus anatum* (formerly *F. anatum,* i.e. regarded as a distinct species), and Green-winged teal to *Anas crecca carolinensis.*

The Glossary (iii): the English names

The English name given in the glossary is «standard» in a non-official sense. The BOU check-list, which covers a majority of European species, states the principle clearly: to make «no attempt to change English usage whether by reviving older names (e.g. 'Dunnock') or by introducing new ones (e.g. 'Pied woodpecker') merely on the ground that

[35] Charles Vaurie, *The Birds of the Palaearctic Fauna, A Systematic Reference: Order Passeriformes* (London 1959). Note that Vaurie's reclassification would probably, if logically extended to the Nearctic passerines, make the *Parulidae* and *Vireonidae, Parulinae* and *Vireoninae* respectively, but I have no authority for doing so.
[36] A. Landsborough Thomson, preface to British Ornithologists' Union List Sub-Committee, *Check-list of the Birds of Great Britain and Ireland* (London 1952), p. vi.

these may be thought by some to be more pleasing or more appropriate... the names of common birds are part of the language, and widely used outside the realm of ornithology».[37] But I am not sure that this list does not occasionally indulge in minor eccentricity, e.g. «Redbreast» for Robin, and I have myself used the names I believe to be in most common use, employing two where they appear to be of approximately equal currency.

On the English and American synonymy I have more to say below, in connection with the Index of English names.

The Glossary (iv): the Spanish names

The English name is then followed by all the Spanish names I have been able to collect and identify with some degree of certainty. The first name cited is always the now official name, and the Spanish names are grouped thereafter in etymological and semantic families. I have exploited all the ornithological sources systematically: the Spanish check-list, the translation of the *Field-guide,* and Jørgensen's two dictionaries, which all supply book-names, and Lletget and the various English orni-thologists, who supply popular names. The Espasa-Calpe encyclopaedia I have tried to use exhaustively, but cannot guarantee that an entry under some obscure heading has not been overlooked. The dictionaries I cite have not been exploited in as thorough-going a fashion, primarily because bird-names listed there are frequently unidentifiable. Dubious identifications, which arise only with the dictionaries, are marked by a question-mark *preceding* the index-letter of the source (thus: ?A).

Unacceptable names are enclosed within oblique strokes. I have pre-ferred to list these terms thus, rather than exclude them, for various reasons. I find them unacceptable for various reasons also. They are of four main kinds: (i) a distinctive name reported by a reliable ornitho-logist for the wrong bird (*cernícalo* for Sparrow-hawk) where it would appear that the error is the informant's;[38] (ii) the scientific Latin name, used by a Spanish ornithologist when no Spanish name was available, and mistakenly recorded by Jørgensen as Spanish: in certain cases the error is patent *(Thalassidroma leucorrhoa),* in others it is impossible to determine whether we have the same kind of error or not *(Fuligula marila)* and I have not marked such cases as unacceptable; (iii) local Catalan names recorded as «Spanish»; I have marked only those phoneti-cally impossible in Castilian; they may be of interest to the student of Catalan and may serve as a reminder that others are also suspect: the Academy's *oliva* (synonymous with *lechuza)* is pure Catalan (v. Corominas); (iv) an obviously inapplicable name, such as *doradillo* for *Motacilla alba: doradillo* must surely indicate a bird with a bit of yellow

---

[37] *Ibid.,* p. v.
[38] It was primarily Dr Evans's observations *(v. supra)* on the names for Kestrel and Sparrow-hawk which persuaded me to exercise no private censorship in any of these doubtful cases.

about it, but *Motacilla alba* is white and black. Other names, also dubious, like *trepatorres* for the Fan-tailed warbler, essentially a country bird, I have not marked as completely unacceptable, but have noted my reservations in Part II of the Glossary.

I have effected various emendations in the spelling of the Spanish names. Jørgensen is appallingly misprinted, though the errors may derive from the source-material, and I have eliminated unnecessary or impossible accents (*cañaméra, trépatroncos*), inserted those necessary (*martin pescador*) and changed grave to acute (*paloma montès*). I have not otherwise emended her spelling, which may in certain cases indicate that we have to do with Latin or Catalan rather than Spanish. Lletget is also, as I have said, sadly misprinted. The most obvious and certain errors I have emended; in other cases I have suggested emendations in parentheses. The English of the English ornithologists is not misprinted, but their Spanish was in most cases scanty, and we have a number of phonetic spellings: Andalusian aspirate *h* is often rendered by *j*, which I have allowed to stand, and *b*'s and *v*'s are used, as might be expected, almost indiscriminately. An impossible spelling like *soldiya* I have marked unacceptable, but kept it in, since it is ambiguous (an attempt at *soldía*, or *soldilla*, with *yeísmo*). I have emended consistently only the single *r* in words like *andaríos, alzarabo, colirojo, cagaropa*, etc. Other dubious spellings I allow to stand, suggesting emendations in parentheses. It is fairly certain that a number of words, apart from those I have marked as unacceptable, are phantoms, due to misunderstanding, mishearing, and misspelling, and sometimes perhaps all three. But I have preferred to put all the cards on the table to allow the reader to arrive at his own conclusions, which may well be different from mine.

A battery of authorities cited after a given name does not necessarily prove its authenticity. There is a certain amount of cannibalism among the ornithologists as among the bilingual lexicographers: «Irby, Jørgensen, Lletget» may well mean that only Irby actually heard the name in use. I have tried to show the relationship of the sources cited in the annotated list (pp. 32-33).

The Glossary Part II

The second part of the Glossary is basically an alphabetical index of all the names to be found in Part I (with a few additions), together with my opinion, expressed by a battery of abbreviations and symbols, of the nature and value of the evidence. Again I have put in everything, Catalan, Portuguese, Latin, and English, wherever certain authorities have taken these names to be Spanish. (Some Catalanisms are supported by A and V, not to mention E, while the English «sanderling» is registered by P.) I have added, in brackets, bird-names, deriving mainly from Martín Alonso and A, which I have been unable to identify at all, or which, explained by the use of some other vernacular term, would have led to a multiplicity of queried entries in Part I.

24

The names are arranged in strictly alphabetical order (English style: *ch* precedes *ci, ll* is treated as two letters) from the initial letter of the bird's *entire* name, whether this consists of one word or two. Although this means that different kinds of *pico,* for example, are to be found before and after a one-word compound like *picofino,* this system will be found, on balance, to avoid more anomalies (like the separation of *ave fría* and *avefría,* etc., etc.) than it creates.

Standard Spanish ornithological usage now, like English, requires an initial capital for the name of a species, but I have not followed this in either part of the Glossary. The distinction between a specific and a non-specific name (except in the official names) is by no means clear in Spanish, and even names which appear only once in Part I may in fact be non-specific. Specific names are indexed to a number in Part I of the Glossary, which not only saves a great deal of space but allows the reader to compare the currency of other terms for the same bird; non-specific names are translated, and indexed to figures which show to which group they refer.

I have added comments of various kinds. I have indicated what I believe or suspect to be now purely book-names, dictionary-words with no popular currency; but it is important to make it clear that this represents an opinion, a well-founded suspicion, and is certainly not a categorical assertion. I have also made frequent use of the annotation «scientific Latin» (which often embraces scientific Greek). Like «book-name» this is a comment which I have overdone rather than underdone. If a bird has some striking characteristic, it is natural that this should be referred to in the scientific Latin, the English name, and the Spanish, but the coincidence of Latin and Spanish is always suspicious, and since the scientific Latin which may lie at the origin of the Spanish is often not the Latin name of modern usage, I thought it prudent at least to note this coincidence.

The late Vicens Vives once made the nice point that the map of the distribution of prehistoric sites in Spain corresponds with that of the universities with departments of archaeology,[39] and the reader, noting the frequency of my annotation «Andalusia, plus?» may wonder (I wonder too) whether the eccentric English captains and colonels, like Verner and Irby, who sallied forth from Gibraltar to watch Andalusian birds, have not imparted an unwarranted southern bias to this list. On the other hand, the bird-population of Spain is distributed (for much the same reasons) very like the pre-Roman human population: predominantly in Andalusia and the Levant, and, more thinly, along the northern coast and mountains. Outside the sierras, which Lilford and Saunders did explore, Castile is, comparatively speaking, an avian desert; and Andalusia, particularly Las Marismas, is still the Mecca of ornithologists from all over Europe. The large number of Catalanisms require special comment. From the nineteenth century on, Catalans have shown themselves

[39] J. Vicens Vives, *Aproximación a la historia de España,* revised ed. (Barcelona 1960), p. 221.

more interested in birds than Castilians; some of my sources (E, J[1], Ll,
V, B) tend to show a Catalan bias (though Gili y Gaya and Corominas
eliminate rather than introduce Catalanisms); and the now official
terminology contains many pure Catalan words, imported to fill the gaps
of Castilian. In short, an Andalusian and Catalan bias does exist in
this Glossary, and I am not sure whether it is wholly justified by the
facts.

The gender of the names *is not noted,* except in the case of the
handful of exceptions [40] to the following rules: overriding all other con-
siderations, if the name is made up of verb plus noun, it is masculine.
Names ending in *-e, -i, -l, -n, -o, -r, -s,* are masculine; those ending in
-a and *-z* are feminine. In some cases there is conflict between the Academy's ruling, and official ornithological usage which tends to regularize
and rationalize gender, making, for example, *barnacla* feminine, and *chotacabras* masculine. I have followed ornithological practice. But for
the bulk of the names listed in the Appendix of unrecorded names one
can only make assumptions. The English ornithologists who provide
most of this material are totally oblivious of the strange device of
grammatical gender (and not alone: Jørgensen and even Lletget do the
same) and are satisfied to write, baldly, the «name».

Some further explanations of Part II of the Glossary will be found
under the explanation of the abbreviations and symbols employed.

The Appendix of names not recorded in Spanish dictionaries

It seemed worthwhile to check the final list of names against the
«diccionario total» of Martín Alonso, [41] which I gave up trying to use
as a source for the Glossary since, without Latin names or detailed
descriptions, his birds are usually unidentifiable. I checked the list at
the same time against Portuguese and Catalan dictionaries to eliminate
lusismos and Catalanisms. [42] The original list of 415 names not
(seemingly) Portuguese or Catalan, was reduced to 388 by further checking
via Romera-Navarro's *Registro* [43] (six names disappeared from the list
completely and a few others moved to the asterisked category), and
V (twelve names), Co, P, and A together eliminated nineteen, while the
DHLE accounted for two more. I do not guarantee that this list could
not be further reduced.

The asterisked entries are good Spanish words (*capitán, coquinero,
mosquitero, sacristán,* etc.) which have not been recorded as the names

---

[40] Ave, aguanieve, aguzanieve; aguanieves, aguzanieves; bisbita, limícola, troglodita; alcatraz, chamariz, malviz.

[41] Martín Alonso, *Enciclopedia del idioma: diccionario histórico y moderno de
la lengua española (siglos XII al XX), etimológico, tecnológico, regional e hispanoame-
ricano,* 3 vols (Madrid 1958).

[42] Primarily, for Portuguese, Morais, *Grande dicionário da língua portuguesa,*
10th ed., 12 vols (Lisbon 1948-1958), and for Catalan, A. M. Alcover and F. de B. Moll,
Diccionari català-valencià-balear, 10 vols (Palma de Mallorca 1952-1962).

[43] M. Romera-Navarro, *Registro de lexicografía hispánica* (Madrid 1951).

of birds. I have not included in this list the quite frequent cases in which a bird-word is explained in the dictionaries as a term used in Peru or Honduras for some exotic species when in fact the word is current in Spain for a Spanish bird. I have not asterisked the words which *do* occur in Spanish dictionaries but which are clearly totally unrelated etymologically to the bird-word (e. g. *ralo<rallus* is not asterisked, although, of course, *ralo<rarus* exists).

The unasterisked list requires more comment. It also contains a number of perfectly good Castilian words (*curita, pastorcilla, soldadito,* etc.) which do not figure in the dictionaries because of the habitual exclusion of diminutives which have no more than diminutive force. It indubitably includes also a number of phantoms, due to mishearing, misunderstanding, misprinting, phonetic rendering of Andaluz pronunciation, and so on, and in Part II of the Glossary I have indicated those names which to me appear suspect. It contains a number of terms which are simply hispanicized scientific Latin. But if *pirrocórax* warrants a place in the dictionaries, why not *nicticórax*? if *falcinelo,* why not *morinelo*? if *álcido,* why not *ampélido*? It contains a number of Catalanisms. But words like *buscarla, fumarel,* and *grévol* are now official Spanish names which will surely find a place in future dictionaries, while terms orthographically and phonologically Castilian, which have clear congeners in Catalan (noted in Part II of the Glossary) may possibly be Aragonese or Murcian. Some involve only the pluralization of the second element of a verb-plus-noun compound, like *becafigos;* some show only a shift of gender from that of the recorded word (*garrapatera, zarzalera,* etc.) and may be misprints; some are merely the qualifier of a recognized compound used without the non-specific (*culebrera* for *águila culebrera, diablo* for *pájaro diablo,* etc.). But even after removing all the doubtful words, Latin, Catalan, phonetically-spelled Andaluz, probable misprints, and what may be the inventions of the official terminology (*coliazul, correlimos,* etc.), there remains a very substantial residue of perfectly plausible Spanish words (*boñiguero, picabueyes,* etc., etc.) the authenticity of which there is no reason to doubt and the existence of which may ultimately be recognized—perhaps by the *DHLE.*

The Index of English names

For the index of English names I have adopted the unusual course of arranging all the names in strict alphabetical order from the first letter of the name, without inversion of qualifier and non-specific. Because Part I of the Glossary groups together eagles, gulls, owls, warblers, etc. and non-specifics are entered in this list indexed to the relevant group, nothing is lost by this procedure, names can be found just as easily, and certain benefits accrue. Besides obviating the complications arising from the erratic hyphenation and compounding of English bird-names (cf. «Grey lag-goose», «Grey-lag goose», «Greylag», etc.), the system has advantages similar to those of a «dictionary in reverse» and throws the most frequent patterns of qualifiers («Red-headed», etc.) into relief.

A name with an initial capital, indicating a species («Snipe»), precedes the name with a lower-case initial indicating a non-specific («snipe»), though all non-specifics are given in the plural and so are usually marked by -s. British English names precede American homonyms indicating distinct species («Robin», «Sparrow-hawk»). Occasionally one or more names may be listed together, if they occur in alphabetical sequence, indexed to one figure (cf. «Andalusian bush-quail», etc.): the «standard» term can in such cases be found by reference to Part I of the Glossary. The entries of non-specific names (eagles, geese, etc.) remove the necessity for listing names in reverse order: «warbler, grasshopper, Pallas's» (or worse), and only names which incorporate scientifically inaccurate non-specifics escape the system. «Cape-pigeon» will not be found under «pigeon», since it is a petrel, so that the lexicographer must still work out his own dictionary-entries.

The primary entries consist of a «standard» name indexed by a figure to Part I of the Glossary, where, usually, a selection of Spanish names can be found. I have provided no easy way from the scientific Latin or the Spanish, to English names other than the standard name. (Bilingual dictionaries are habitually overburdened by lists of obsolete English synonyms, «goatsucker, fern-owl, churn-owl», etc., which can serve only to mislead.) And the lexicographer will need to use in addition Part II of the Glossary, in order to see how far popular names, which should clearly in general be preferred to invented book-names, are ambiguous. There are three other types of entry: the English «generic» names indexed to the birds covered by the term, specific names followed by «v. also» which indicates the existence of other specific names incorporating the specific cited (thus under «Black-headed gull» the reader is referred also to «Mediterranean black-headed gull» and «Great black-headed gull»), and synonyms.

The list of synonyms could have been expanded enormously, to some six thousand entries, by using the various dictionaries of English ornithological synonyms (see p. 5, note 12), but whether a completely exhaustive *bilingual* dictionary is either necessary or desirable is highly debatable. I have therefore confined the selection of synonyms to the following categories: (i) names which occur with fair frequency in modern English ornithological literature not accepted by the BOU check-list, and also official BOU names (one or two only) which I have not accepted as standard; (ii) the names given by the various nineteenth-century sources I have used (here identification, given the antique scientific Latin, might be very difficult for someone who wanted to refer to the literature I have used); (iii) the most common of the obsolete literary («poetic») and popular names («glead», «goatsucker», «nun», etc.); and finally (iv) American synonyms.

The American synonymy is not easy to handle. Coincidence of species between the Palaearctic and Nearctic regions occurs largely among the non-passeres, and among far-flying water-birds, gulls, waders, petrels, divers, and so on. Even so, the American species is not often identical with the European, and whether the two obviously related species are in fact conspecific is often in debate. I have already cited the examples of the Peregrine and the Teal. Though these subspecies were once accounted distinct species it has long been agreed that they are conspecific. But the proposed lumping of *Bubo virginianus* and *Bubo bubo* is more recent, and the discussion goes on. This means that, when American English is equated with British English, we may have to do with two distinct subspecies (which is not finally of great importance), and also that American birds not listed here may, with further lumping, have ready-made Spanish names. But American lexicographers have still various problems to solve, and there are various sources of error. Often Americans give English names to different American birds. This is a very well-known phenomenon of colonial linguistics, and occurs also with Spanish names in Latin America. (And of course the same ambiguities arise with Australian English.) Sometimes we have to do with quite different birds: «Robin», «Sparrow-hawk», «Avocet», etc. and the synonyms create further confusion. American «Screech-owl» is not a synonym for the Barn-owl but the name of a distinct species, *Otus asio,* and a non-specific for members of the genus *Otus.* «Horned owl» also indicates different birds, as I have mentioned. On the other hand some American names are English names «correctly» applied to the identical species encountered on the other side of the Atlantic also. (All these problems arise also with Spanish and Spanish American names, with the added complication that there exists no official Spanish check-list for the whole of the New-world avifauna.)

Many common English synonyms are paired. This is concealed in this Glossary. But it should be noted that one does not employ «Brown linnet» alongside «Greenfinch», but with «Green linnet». Cf. also Black cormorant = Cormorant/Green cormorant = Shag; Green-winged teal (Am.) = Teal/Blue-winged teal (Am. and British English). One final point about the synonyms: I have consistently eliminated the American synonyms used by certain American ornithologists who follow the extraordinary practice of eliminating the possessive: Sabine gull, Wilson petrel, etc.

The lexicographer's task

Spanish lexicographers and etymologists [44] will know how to deal with the evidence presented here, but for the bilingual lexicographer this Glossary is still very far from being the answer to that harmless drudge's prayers.

The Spanish-English bilingual lexicographer has to cope, so far as vernacular zoological nomenclature is concerned, with at least four

---

[44] I have not here attempted to list the proposed etymologies which reliable identifications make suspect. The etymologist should look at the pictures in B², where among other things, he will find a *carlanco (carraca)* to be collarless (cf. Co s. v. CARLANCA).

dialects, British and American English, and Peninsular and American Spanish. The confusion of the four (among other factors) leads to break-down, that «gran confusión que reina en los diccionarios bilingües» of which Corominas writes. And although the list of American synonyms included in the Index of English names may serve to clear up one or two difficulties, further lists and glossaries are required: a list of the British and American homonyms for distinct species, a list of the Peninsular and American Spanish hononyms (I have noted a few in Part II), and, above all, a glossary of American Spanish bird-names, reliably identified. Without a coherent total view of all Spanish bird-names we shall have, if not error, only partial truths. And it should go without saying that unless the lexicographer is prepared to express his doubts and uncertainties («?») he must try to get rid of the rash of question-marks which afflicts Part II of my Glossary.

The bilingual lexicographer must learn also to curb his natural desire to establish a one-to-one correspondence between Spanish and English when the semantic areas of non-specifics, such as «águila» and «eagle», do not coincide; to accept that one-word names are in the vast majority non-specific; and to admit a great many more complex names, non-specific plus qualifier, to his list of «words».

One obvious problem which faces the compiler of a bilingual dictionary is the selection of entries. The accepted criterion is normally frequency of occurrence, but bird-names, except for the most common, fall outside the scope of word-counts. And the commonness or otherwise of the bird itself is no criterion at all. In England, for instance, the Knot probably outnumbers the Kingfisher by some one hundred thousand to one; but whereas everyone knows the Kingfisher, far fewer people know the Knot. The average non-expert Englishman could certainly pick an adequate English-Spanish list, but would probably discard, in the Spanish-English section, «Andalusian hemipode», «Bonelli's eagle», «Rufous bush-warbler», and «Fan-tailed warbler». In a short dictionary, the lexicographer, even selecting the most frequent Spanish bird-words, would wind up with a rather eccentric selection if he insisted on reproducing only his English entries in the Spanish section and *vice versa*. It is a question of distribution; whole orders of birds (grebes, divers, grouse, and so on) are predominantly northern, while others (hoopoes, bee-eaters, rollers) are southern. One of the many things wrong with existing bilingual dictionaries is that the compilers have omitted comparatively common Spanish bird-words, possibly, one suspects, because of the outlandish English translation: «Black-bellied sand-grouse», «Collared pratincole», «Short-toed lark», etc.

The translator, as distinct from the lexicographer, might best solve the very rare problems of this kind by retaining the Spanish: *torillo, ortega,* etc., or by eliminating the qualifier and rendering *torillo* as «button-quail», *ortega* as «sand-grouse». The translator may also meet with the problem of translating names (of birds, beetles, butterflies or fish) for which no Spanish equivalent exists at all. I find in one polyglot technical journal [45] a passage in Spanish which has in successive lines «el Eskimo curlew», «la Whooping crane», «el Everglade kite». (It is true that all three are very rare, and American, but being on the verge of extinction they are perhaps even more frequently referred to than commoner birds.) This blatant *extranjerismo* is a curious solution of the difficulty: the scientific Latin or even an *ad hoc* coinage (*zarapito esquimal*, now the official name, would have been easy, acceptable, and unequivocal) would seem to provide a better solution.

As Williams has noted *(op. cit.)* «linguists will for a long time to come be asked to supervise the making of dictionaries, even though they have to cooperate with technicians in every field of knowledge to make them». Lexicographers inexpert in ornithology become, as we have seen, hopelessly confused, even when quite patently using technical literature; on the other hand the hispanist will not long repress a shudder in the face of an ornithologist's «dictionary» such as J^1. One suspects that the cooperation of a «technician» and a «linguist» might still be bedevilled by misunderstandings; and that what we need are hispanist-icthyologists, hispanist-lepidopterists, hispanist-botanists, and so on. We have still a very long way to go before we have enough adequate micro-glossaries for Spanish and English; this Glossary represents no more than a stage towards the construction of one of them.

[45] *Bulletin of the International Committee for Bird Preservation*, VI (1952), pp. 232-233.

ABBREVIATIONS AND SYMBOLS

Glossary Part I

A = Real Academia Española, *Diccionario de la lengua española,* 17th and 18th eds (Madrid 1948 and 1956). Where entries differ they are distinguished as A48 and A56.

B = B¹ and B².
B¹ = Francisco Bernís, *Prontuario de la avifauna española (incluyendo aves de Portugal, Baleares y Canarias) con los nombres científicos y españoles aprobados por la comisión: Lista patrón de la Sociedad Española de Ornitología,* separata of *Ardeola,* I (1955).
B² = *Guía de campo de las aves de España y demás países de Europa* (Madrid 1957), the Spanish version, by Mauricio González Díez, of Roger Peterson, Guy Mountfort, and P. A. D. Hollom, *Field-guide to the Birds of Europe* (London 1954). The additional Spanish names were devised with the advice of Bernís.

C. C¹ = Abel Chapman, 'Rough notes on Spanish ornithology', *Ibis,* 1884, pp. 66-69.
C² = Abel Chapman, 'Winter notes in Spain', *Ibis,* 1888, pp. 444-461.
C³ = Abel Chapman and Walter C. Buck, *Wild Spain: España Agreste* (London 1893), especially pp. 457-459.
C⁴ = Abel Chapman and Walter C. Buck, *Unexplored Spain* (London 1910).

Co = Joan Corominas, *Diccionario crítico etimológico de la lengua castellana,* 4 vols (Berne 1954). (Very infrequently cited.)

D = *Duden español, diccionario por la imagen* (London 1963).

E = *Enciclopedia universal ilustrada europeo-americana,* 70+10+6 vols, Espasa-Calpe (Madrid-Barcelona s. a.).

I = Lt-Col L. H. Irby, *The Ornithology of the Strait of Gibraltar,* 2nd revised and enlarged ed. (London 1895). (First ed. London 1875). (Irby also supplies Moroccan Arabic names.)

J = J¹ and J².
J¹ = Harriet I. Jørgensen and Cecil I. Blackburne, *Glossarium Europae avium* (Copenhagen 1941). (Seventeen languages are represented. The Spanish bird-names derive from Arévalo y Baca, Ventura de los Reyes, and a correspondent Sr Luis Iglesias of Santiago. See p. 6, note 14).
J² = Harriet I. Jørgensen, *Nomina avium europaearum* (Copenhagen 1958). (Based on J¹, B, Ll, and Angel Cabrera, *Las aves. Historia natural,* I: *Zoología,* Barcelona s. a. The assistance of Bernís is also acknowledged.)

Jo = F. C. R. Jourdain, 'The birds of southern Spain: Part I, Passeres', *Ibis,* 1936, 725-763; 'Part II, Passeres', *ibid.,* 1937, 110-152 (unfinished). (Many names appear to derive from Irby and Saunders.)

L = Lord Lilford, 'Notes on the ornithology of Spain', *Ibis,* 1865, pp. 166-177; *ibid.,* 1866, 173-187; *ibid.,* 1866, 377-392. (Most of the material comes from central Castile.)

Le = A. Starker Leopold, *Wild-life of Mexico: the Game-birds and Mammals* (Berkeley and Los Angeles 1959).

Ll = Augusto Gil Lletget, *Sinopsis de las aves de España y Portugal* (Madrid 1945). (Frequent citation of I, L, and S may mean that some of the names recorded derive from these sources, and were not noted independently; he has also used Martínez Gámez, *Ornitología andaluza y de España en general,* Madrid 1906, a work I have been unable to see.)

M = Guy Mountfort, 'The larks of Andalusia', *Ibis,* 1954, 111-115.

N = H. Noble, 'Forty-four days' nesting in Andalucia', *Ibis,* 1902, 69-89.

P = Miguel Toro y Gisbert, *Pequeño Larousse ilustrado* (Paris 1940).

R = W. H. Riddell, 'Field-notes from observations in Spain on birds on the British list', *Ibis,* 1945, 408-422.

S. S¹ = Howard Saunders, 'Ornithological rambles in Spain', *Ibis,* 1869, 170-195. S (no superscript figure) = Howard Saunders, 'A list of the birds of southern Spain', *Ibis,* 1871, 54-68; *ibid.,* 205-225; *ibid.,* 384-402.

Sn = D. W. Snow *et alii,* 'Land- and sea-bird migration in North Western Spain, Autumn 1954', *Ibis,* 1955, 557-572.

So = Sociedad Española de Ornitología, *Bases para un proyecto de clasificación legal de las aves de España,* separata of *Ardeola,* III (1956). (There are only a very few minor changes from B¹.)

T = C. B. Ticehurst and H. Whistler, 'On the avifauna of Galicia', *Ibis,* 1928, 663-683.

V = Samuel Gili y Gaya, *Vox: Diccionario general ilustrado de la lengua española,* revised ed. (Barcelona 1956).

Ve = Willoughby Verner, *My Life among the Wild Birds in Spain* (London 1909). (Confined to Andalusia.)

/Oblique strokes/ enclosing a name indicate that it is unacceptable (not Spanish, or wrongly, but positively, identified). Why the word is unacceptable will be indicated in Part II of the Glossary.

(Parentheses) mark my suggested emendation of an unacceptable or otherwise dubious word.

? *preceding* an authority (usually a dictionary) indicates that this identification is uncertain.

Glossary Part II

Am America, American Spanish.

Andal Andalusia, Andalusian. I take it that all other geographical abbreviations need no further explanation: Arag, Ast, Cast, Cat, Gal, Mex, Murc, etc.

arch archaic. A medieval or later name which continues to live in the dictionaries but does not appear to have any modern popular currency.

bkn book-name, a name which appears to have no popular currency, but is confined to the *technical* literature (cf. «poet»).

conf confusion, confused with.

Eng English.

esp especially.

etym etymology, etymologically.

f (1) feminine gender (only the exceptions to the rules given on p. 26 are noted); (2) female of.

fam family.

Fr French.

gen genus, genera, generic.

gen−, gen+ the word, usually originally intended to be generic, now, because of changes in the taxonomy, covers less, or more, than a genus; alternatively, gen−, to one very distinctive member of this genus, this generic term is never applied.

gen², ³ etc. applied to two, threee, etc. genera.

gen/fam in Part I of the Glossary, i.e. in Europe, a family is represented by only one genus. The non-specific in question may apply only to the genus or to the whole family.

improp improper, improperly.

improp sp improperly specific, i.e. the word is a non-specific and should not be treated as though it applied to a single species.

Lat Latin. A learned word deriving from the Latin, not annotated «scl» inasmuch as its currency antedates the establishment of the Linnaean system.

m (1) masculine gender (only the exceptions to the rules given on p. 26 are noted); (2) male of.

mispr misprint, misprint for.

nonsp non-specific (see note 10).

nonsp/gen popular usage of the non-specific coincides with ornithological usage of the term as a generic, i.e. popular perception of relationship is supported by the scientific evidence.

off official name. If this is not also marked «pop» it may be suspected to be a book-name or an invention.

orthog orthographical.

poet poetic literary usage, neither popular nor technical.

reg regional. Not in general use but current either in more than one dialect area or in an undetermined area.

reg var   regional dialectal variant of.

scl   scientific Latin. The non-specific or the qualifier, or both, coincides etymologically or semantically with, and may be suspected to be a hispanicization or translation of, the modern or an older scientific Latin name, e.g. *pufino de los ingleses (Puffinus anglorum)*.

sp   species, specific, used specifically.

subfam   subfamily.

v.   *vide,* see.

var   variant of. This refers the reader to the more usual form, and is sometimes rather loosely employed, e.g. «*ave zonza* var *ave tonta*».

/Oblique strokes/   round a main entry indicate that the word is not Spanish; round an index-figure, indicate that the name is incorrectly applied to this bird.

/?/   between a main entry and an index-figure means either (1) that the name is suspect: phonologically improbable for Castilian, or an unrecorded name easily assimilable to a better-known name by postulating an error of mishearing, misunderstanding, misprinting, etc.; (2) that the identification is doubtful. The nature of the suspicion is always indicated by some further annotation.

?   The question-mark is used very precisely to query *only* the immediately preceding word or symbol. So «Andal +?» means that the name is definitely current in Andalusia, and may be current elsewhere; «131 +?» means that the name certainly attaches to No. 131 but may be applied to other birds; «improp? sp»: «is this word improperly specific?» (there is no doubt that the source uses it specifically); «serrata mispr? serreta»: «is this a misprint for 'serreta'?» («serreta» is an amply attested word). A space before the question-mark leaves the query to stand as the sign of an unknown quantity; «pardón Ast falcon ?» means that «falcon» is not queried, but which particular species is intended is in doubt.

(?)   marks a less grave doubt than «?».

(Parentheses)   mark guesses or emendations for which Part I provides some evidence.

[Brackets]   mark (1) entries not included, for reasons explained above, in Part I. Without some specific indication to the contrary, all such entries derive from Martín Alonso, who, of course, leans heavily on such works as A. (The identification of a bracketed main entry is never unequivocal and should be treated with great caution: without the scientific Latin or a description with differentiating detail one can only guess, and it is all too easy to suppose, for example, that a «pájaro tonto» must be the same as a «pájaro bobo».) (2) other information not entered in Part I of the Glossary.

+   plus and − minus signs should be self-explanatory «Burgos Sant +?»: the name is current in Northern Castile and may have wider currency; «207+»: the name appears as an entry under 207 but must also apply to other birds; «zarcero ... warblers (−)»: zarcero covers a smaller semantic area than the English «warbler», but no better non-specific translation is available; «correlimos ... stints (+)»: correlimos covers a larger semantic area than «stint».

±   the semantic areas of the English and Spanish non-specifics overlap and neither is entirely included within the other.

Consecutive index-figures separated by a hyphen, e.g. 357-358, indicate that the birds belong to the same genus and that the word is probably a non-specific; separated by commas, they are of different species and are otherwise dissimilar, so that some confusion or error may be suspected.

An illustration or two may help to make things clearer:

chirlomirlo   (1) /?/491 [490?]; (2) [Sal=tordo ?]

means that *chirlomirlo* appears in Part I under 491 (which will be found to be *mirlo,* Blackbird, and an identification supported only by P) but that I am doubtful of this, and suggest 490 (under which entry *chirlo* will be found to be a well-attested popular word for the Ring-ouzel); one of the dictionaries says it is used in Salamanca to mean «*tordo*», but what *tordo* means I do not know.

milano   (1) off pop nonsp/gen 125-126 kites; (2) pop sp 125; (3) pop conf? improp? sp 131, cf. milano blanco, nonsp? 131-134 harriers; (4) error? 124, but cf. milano jaspeado, nonsp? 122-124 hawks

means (1) that *milano* is a non-specific in popular, and now official, use for the kites; (2) as a specific in popular use the bird intended is 125; (3) the name is noted also for 131, but I wonder whether there is some confusion here—it would not be difficult to mistake a Marsh-harrier (131) for a Kite, without a clear view of the tail; on the other hand *milano blanco* (and *milano gris*) is also recorded, for 132, and I wonder whether the term is a non-specific applied to the harriers also; (4) *milano* is also identified (by A and V) as 124 (the Goshawk), which is much more likely to be an error; on the other hand Irby heard «*milano jaspeado*» for the Sparrow-hawk, and I wonder whether *milano* may not be a non-specific for the hawks also.

Glossary: Part I

GAVIIFORMES

GAVIIDAE

1. Gavia arctica (Black-throated diver): colimbo ártico BJ^2; colimbo menor J; /pájaro bobo/, /pingüino/V.
2. Gavia immer (Great northern diver): colimbo grande BJ^2; colimbo glacial J.
3. Gavia adamsii (White-billed diver): colimbo de Adams B^2J^2.
4. Gavia stellata (Red-throated diver): colimbo chico BJ^2; /cadellot/J; /cabrellot/blanco J^1; /cabrellot blanc/J^2.

PODICIPIDIFORMES

PODICIPIDIDAE

5. Podiceps cristatus (Great crested grebe): somormujo lavanco BJ^2; somormujo moñudo EJ; somorgujo EV; zambullidor LlJ^2; zaramagullón V.
6. Podiceps griseigena (Red-necked grebe): somormujo cuellirrojo BJ^2; somormujo de mejillas grises J.
7. Podiceps auritus (Slavonian grebe): zampullín cuellirrojo BJ^2; zampullín orejudo J^2; somormujo orejudo J; noveleta cuellirroja J^2.
8. Podiceps caspicus (Black-necked grebe): zampullín cuellinegro BJ^2; somormujo de cuello negro J; noveleta cuellinegra J^2; somorgujo, zaramagullón ?A.
9. Podiceps ruficollis (Little grebe): zampullín chico, zampullín común BJ^2; somormujo menor, somormujo pequeño EJ; somormujo castaño E.

PROCELLARIIFORMES

DIOMEDEIDAE

10. Diomedea exulans (Wandering albatross): albatros viajero B^2J^2; albatros común EJ^2; albatros E?A; carnero del Cabo E.
11. Diomedea melanophrys (Black-browed albatross): albatros ojeroso B^2J^2; albatros de párpados negros E.
12. Diomedea chlororhynchos (Yellow-nosed albatross): albatros clororrinco B^2J^2; albatros de pico amarillo E.
13. Diomedea chrysostoma (Grey-headed albatross): albatros cabecigrís B^2J^2.
14. Phoebetria palpebrata (Light-mantled sooty albatross): albatros sombrío B^2J^2.

PROCELLARIIDAE

15. Oceanites oceanicus (Wilson's petrel): paíño de Wilson B^2; paíño de Wilson B^1J^2; petrel J^2; /thalassidroma oceanica/J^1.
16. Oceanodroma leucorrhoa (Leach's petrel): paíño de Leach B^2; paíño de Leach B^1J^2; /thalassidroma leucorrhoa/J^1.
17. Oceanodroma castro (Madeiran petrel): paíño de Madeira B^2; paíño de Madeira B^1J^2.
18. Hydrobates pelagicus (Storm-petrel): paíño común B^2; paíño común B^1J^2; ave de San Pedro E; ave de las tempestades JV; petrel EJ?AV.
19. Pelagodroma marina (Frigate-petrel): paíño pechialbo B^2; paíño pechialbo B^1J^2.
20. Procellaria puffinus (Manx shearwater): pardela pichoneta BJ^2; fardela del Atlántico, pufino de los ingleses J; ánima, diablo SI; patín A?V.
    20a. P. p. puffinus (Manx shearwater): pardela pichoneta inglesa B^1.
    20b. P. p. yelkouan (Levantine shearwater): pardela pichoneta yelkouan B^1.
    20c. P. p. mauretanicus (West Mediterranean shearwater): pardela pichoneta balear B.

21. Procellaria baroli (Little shearwater): pardela chica BJ².
22. Procellaria lherminieri (Audubon's shearwater): pardela de Audubon B²J².
23. Procellaria gravis (Great shearwater): pardela capirotada BJ².
24. Procellaria diomedea (see subspecies): pardela cenicienta BJ²; fardela del Mediterráneo J.
    P. d. diomedea (Mediterranean shearwater).
    P. d. borealis (North Atlantic shearwater).
25. Procellaria grisea (Sooty shearwater): pardela sombría BJ².
26. Bulweria bulwerii (Bulwer's petrel): petrel de Bulwer BJ².
27. Bulweria neglecta (Kermadec petrel): petrel de Kermadec B²J²
28. Bulweria leucoptera (Collared petrel): petrel aliblanco B²J².
29. Bulweria hasitata (Black-capped petrel): petrel diablotín B²J².
30. Daption capensis (Cape-pigeon): paloma del Cabo B²J².
31. Fulmarus glacialis (Fulmar): fulmar BJ; fulmar europeo E; fulmar glacial D.

PELECANIFORMES

SULIDAE

32. Sula bassana (Gannet): alcatraz común DBJ²; alcatraz IEJ¹Ll; bubía E; sula loca D.

PHALACROCORACIDAE

33. Phalacrocorax carbo (Cormorant): cormorán grande BJ²; gran cormorán J¹; cormorán común ED; cormorán EA; cormorano P; cuervo marino SIEJLlAPV; cuervo de mar E; corvejón V; mergo, mergánsar EAPV.
    33a. P. c. carbo (Cormorant): cormorán grande nórdico B¹.
    33b. P. c. sinensis (Southern cormorant): cormorán grande chino B¹.
34. Phalacrocorax aristotelis (Shag): cormorán moñudo EJB; cuervo marino moñudo J¹.
    34a. P. a. aristotelis (Shag): cormorán moñudo atlántico B¹.
    34b. P. a. desmarestii (—): cormorán moñudo sardo B¹.
35. Phalacrocorax pygmaeus (Pygmy cormorant): cormorán pigmeo B²J²; cormorán enano J.

41

FREGATIDAE

36. Fregata magnificens (Magnificent man-o'-war bird): rabihorcado grande B^2J^2; rabihorcado común E; rabihorcado ?A?PV; fragata E; pájaro burro V.

PELECANIDAE

37. Pelecanus onocrotalus (White pelican): pelícano vulgar BJ^2; pelícano común J^1; pelícano ELlAPV; pelicano V; alcatraz E; /platalea/V.
38. Pelecanus crispus (Dalmatian pelican): pelícano ceñudo B^2J^2.

ARDEIFORMES

ARDEIDAE

39. Ardea cinerea (Heron): garza real SEJAPVB; garza común ED; garza cristada J; garza real cenicienta ED; garza ceniza I; garza gris LlJ^2; garza $ILlJ^2$; pella E; airón APV.
40. Ardea purpurea (Purple heron): garza imperial EBJ^2; garza real purpúrea, garza purpúrea J^1; garza roja E; garza moruna SEJ; garza pardilla J^2; garza $ILlAPVJ^2$.
41. Egretta garzetta (Little egret): garceta común EBJ^2; garceta menor J; garceta AV; garcete E; garza blanca SIJ^2; garzota E; garzota común J^2; cataraña ?A?V.
42. Egretta alba (Large egret): garceta grande BJ^2; garza blanca $SIEJ^1$; garzota grande J^2.
43. Ardeola ralloides (Squacco heron): garcilla cangrejera BJ^2; garza cangrejera EJ^1; cangrejera S?V; garza canaria IJ^1; garza E.
44. Ardeola ibis (Cattle-egret): garcilla bueyera BJ^2; espulgabueyes SEJ; purgabueyes SIVe; picabueyes $ELlJ^2$; garrapatosa IEJ; agarrapatosa C^3; garrapatera LlJ^2; reznero EJ^2; bubulco E.
45. Nycticorax nycticorax (Night-heron): martinete $SIEVBJ^2$; martín del río EV; martín peña E; garza de noche IEJ^2; garza gris I; zumaya EJ^1APV; zumacaya, capacho V; nictícorax E.

46. Ixobrychus minutus (Little bittern): avetorillo común BJ^2;
    cangrejera Ll; cangrejerita S; ardea menor J^1; garza enana J^2.
47. Ixobrychus sturmi (African dwarf bittern): avetorillo de Sturm B^1.
48. Botaurus stellaris (Bittern): avetoro común BJ^2; avetoro SC^{3}J^{1}LlV;
    ave toro, ave-toro E; pájaro toro I; garza mochuelo SC^{1}C^3; garza
    dorada J^1; cangrejera S; guía de las gallinetas I; /alcavarán/E.
49. Botaurus lentiginosus (American bittern): avetoro lentiginoso BJ^2.

CICONIIDAE

50. Ciconia ciconia (White stork): cigüeña común BJ^2; cigüeña blanca
    EJ^2; cigüeña SIC^{3}J^{1}LlAV.
51. Ciconia nigra (Black stork): cigüeña negra SIC^{3}EJLlAB.

PLATALEIDAE

52. Platalea leucorodia (Spoonbill): espátula SIELlPBJ^2; espátula
    blanca J; cuchareta SIELl?VJ^2; ave de cuchar, ave de cuchara E;
    paleto S; paleta, paletón, pilato, patera I; platalea E.
53. Plegadis falcinellus (Glossy ibis): morito SIEJLlAVB; falcinelo
    EAV; falcinelo brillante J^1; garza diablo S.

PHOENICOPTERIFORMES

PHOENICOPTERIDAE

54. Phoenicopterus ruber (Flamingo): flamenco SIEJLlAPVB; flamenco
    rosa E; /picaza marina/EV.

ANSERIFORMES

ANATIDAE

55. Anas platyrhyncha (Mallard): ánade real BJ^2; pato real SIC^{3}J^1;
    ánade, pato AV; ánade vulgar J^1; ánade común E; pato silvestre
    EJ; pato común, pato de collar, pato galán Le; azulón LlJ^2;
    parro EAV; ánade salvaje/collvert/J^2.

43

56. Anas discors (Blue-winged teal): cerceta aliazul B^2J^2; cerceta de alas azules, zarceta de verano, zarceta de otoño, zarceta tulera Le; pato chiquito E.

57. Anas crecca (Teal): cerceta común BJ^2Le; cerceta menor EJ; zarceta menor E; cerceta de invierno J; zarceta de invierno, cerceta de lista verde Le; cerceta SELl; zarceta C^3; sarceta $ILlJ^2$; /sarset/J^2; salseno Le; pato serrano E; patito S.

58. Anas angustirostris (Marbled teal): cerceta pardilla BJ^2; pardilla IC^3LlJ^2; ruhilla IC^3; pato jaspeado S; carretera Ll; roseta J^2.

59. Anas querquedula (Garganey): cerceta carretona BJ^2; cerceta común J^1; cerceta mayor J; cerceta EV; zarceta V; capitán caretón (carretón?) C^3; capitán I; /roncadell/J^2.

60. Anas formosa (Baikal teal): cerceta del Baikal B^2J^2.

61. Anas falcata (Falcated teal): cerceta de alfanjes B^2J^2.

62. Anas strepera (Gadwall): ánade friso BJ^2; friso C^3; frisa $ILlJ^2$; silbón real C^1C^3; pato castellano J; pato pinto, pato cabezón, pato pardo de grupo Le; ascle J^2.

63. Anas penelope (Wigeon): ánade silbón BJ^2; silbón $IC^3EJLl?V$; pato silbador SJ; pato franciscano I; pato real de mar J^1; píulo J^2.

64. Anas americana (Baldpate, American wigeon): ánade silbón americano B^2J^2; pato calvo, pato chalcuán, pato panadero, saradillo, cotorrito Le.

65. Anas acuta (Pintail): ánade rabudo BJ^2; pato rabudo $INLlJ^2$; rabudo $C^2C^3J^2$; pato rabilargo J^1; rabilargo LlJ^2; pato careto I; pato careta, cara de juez LlJ^2; pato pescuecilargo E; pato golondrino (golondrina?), pato de guías, pato floridano Le; /cua de junc/J^2

66. Spatula clypeata (Shoveler): pato cuchara BJ^2; pato cuchareta $SIELlJ^2$; pato cucharetero J^1; pato cucharón, pato cucharudo Le; cuchareta ?V; pato bocón, pato cuaresmeño Le; paletón IC^3ELlJ^2; sardinero IE; espátula común E; espátula ?V; /bragat/J^2.

67. Aix galericulata (Mandarin): pato mandarín EB^2J^2.

68. Netta rufina (Red-crested pochard): pato colorado JB; branta rojiza J^1; /sibert/Ll; /sivert/J^2.

69. Aythya marila (Scaup): porrón bastardo BJ^2; fuligula marila J^1; fulígula gris E; pato bocón, pato boludo Le.

70. Aythya fuligula (Tufted duck): porrón moñudo BJ^2; moñudo LlJ^2; ánade cristado de ribera, fuligula de cresta J^1; fulígula moñuda, pato pelucón E; /negreta/J^2; /morell/, /morell capellut/J^2.

71. Aythya ferina (Pochard): porrón común BJ^2; cenizo IJ; cabezón SIC^3LlJ^2; /boix/J^2.
72. Aythya nyroca (White-eyed pochard): porrón pardo BJ^2; pardote SIJLl; negrete IC^3Ll; fuligula de ojos blancos J^1; /rotget/J^2.
73. Bucephala clangula (Golden-eye): porrón osculado BJ^2; clángula vulgar J^1; pato chillón ojos dorados Le.
74. Bucephala islandica (Barrow's golden-eye): porrón islándico BJ^2.
75. Bucephala albeola (Buffel-head): porrón albeola B^2J^2; pato chillón jorobado, pato monja Le.
76. Clangula hyemalis (Long-tailed duck): /havelda/BJ^2; harelda de los hielos J.
77. Melanitta fusca (Velvet scoter): negrón especulado BJ^2; negreta E?P; negreta de alas blancas Le; /pato negro/A; /morell de mar/J.
78. Melanitta perspicillata (Surf-scoter): negrón careto B^2J^2; negreta, negreta de marejada Le.
79. Melanitta nigra (Common scoter): negrón común BJ^2; pato negro IC^3JLlV; negreta EV; coquinero ILl; fusca ?EV.
80. Histrionicus histrionicus (Harlequin): pato arlequín B^2J^2; clángula histriónico (histriónica?) J^1.
81. Polysticta stelleri (Steller's eider): eider de Steller B^2; negrón de Steller J^2.
82. Somateria mollissima (Eider-duck): eider JPB; eíder V; eider común E; pato de flojel EAV.
83. Somateria spectabilis (King eider): eider real B^2J^2.
84. Somateria fischeri (Spectacled eider): eider de Fischer B^2J^2.
85. Oxyura leucocephala (White-headed duck): malvasía SB^1J^2; malvasia B^2; porrón IC^3LlJ^2; pato porrón C^1C^3; /pato tarro/S; erismaturo leucocéfalo J^1.
86. Mergus cucullatus (Hooded merganser): serreta cabezona B^2J^2; mergo de caperuza, pato rampla Le.
87. Mergus serrator (Red-breasted merganser): serreta mediana BJ^2; serrata J; pato de sierra I; mergo de cresta J; mergo copetón, mergo de pecho oscuro Le.
88. Mergus merganser (Goosander): serreta grande BJ^2; pato sierra DJ; mergo J; mergo americano Le.
89. Mergus albellus (Smew): serreta chica BJ^2; serratilla J.
90. Tadorna tadorna (Sheld-duck): tarro blanco BJ^2; pato tarro SIC^3; anserata I; tadorna de Belon J; tadorna común E.

91. Tadorna ferruginea (Ruddy sheld-duck): tarro canelo BJ^2; pato canelo IC^{3}EJ; pato tarro SI; labanco (lavanco) IC^3.

92. Anser anser (Grey lag-goose): ánsar común BJ^2; ánsar I; ánsar cenizo J^1; ganso cenizo J; ganso ceniciento salvaje E; oca cenicienta J; oca cenicienta salvaje E; ganso bravo SLlJ^2; ganso ILlV.
92a. A. a. anser (Western greylag): ánsar común occidental B^2.
92b. A. a. rubirostris (Eastern greylag): ánsar común oriental B^2.

93. Anser albifrons (White-fronted goose): ánsar careto grande BJ^2; ganso careto, oca de frente blanca J; ganso frente blanca, oca salvaje Le; ánsar frentialbo grande J^2.

94. Anser erythropus (Lesser white-fronted goose): ánsar careto chico BJ^2; ánsar frentialbo chico J^2.

95. Anser arvensis (Bean-goose): ánsar campestre BJ^2; ánsar I; ganso bravo SJ^1; ganso de la mies J; ganso I; oca silvestre J; oca V.

96. Anser brachyrhynchus (Pink-footed goose): ánsar piquicorto BJ^2; oca de pico corto J; ánsar braquirrinco J^2.

97. Anser hyperboreus (Snow-goose): ánsar nival B^{2}J^2; ánsar hiperbóreo J^2; ánsar/blanca/(blanco), ánsar real Le; ganso de las nieves J.

98. Eulabeia indica (Bar-headed goose): ganso peluquín J^2.

99. Cygnopsis cygnoides (Swan-goose): ganso cisnal J^2; /oca asiática/E.

100. Branta bernicla (Brent goose): barnacla carinegra BJ^2; bernacha de collar J.

101. Branta leucopsis (Barnacle-goose): barnacla cariblanca BJ^2; ganso monjita J; ganso de los percebes J^1.

102. Branta canadensis (Canada goose): barnacla canadiense B^{2}J^2; ganso/oca del Canadá ELe; ganso gritón, ganso graznador Le.

103. Branta ruficollis (Red-breasted goose): barnacla cuellirroja B^{2}J^2.

104. Cygnus olor (Mute swan): cisne vulgar BJ^2; cisne común DJ; cisne manso J; cisne mudo D; cisne doméstico ordinario E; cisne SELlVJ^2.

105. Cygnus cygnus (Whooper-swan): cisne cantor EJB; cisne salvaje J; cisne silvestre E; cisne ILl.

106. Cygnus columbianus (Bewick's swan): cisne chico BJ^2; cisne de Bewick JB^2; cisne chiflador Le.

FALCONIFORMES

AEGYPIIDAE

107. Neophron percnopterus (Egyptian vulture): alimoche común BJ^2; alimoche EJ^{1}Ll?V; alimocha LSI; abanto SIE?AV; avanto Ll; quebrantahuesos IC^{3}Ll; boñiguero LlJ^2; rejilero S; pernetero, monigero I; águila blanca L; grajo blanco S; aguiloria J^2; /buitre/J^1.

108. Gyps fulvus (Griffon vulture): buitre común EJB; buitre ILl?AV; buitre franciscano LSI; buitre leonado J; pajaraco I.

109. Aegypius monachus (Black vulture): buitre negro LSIEJLlAB; buitre monje JA; /buitre franciscano/A; /abanto/J; /rejilero/S^1.

110. Gypaëtus barbatus (Bearded vulture): quebrantahuesos LSIC^{3}EJLl AVB; quebrantón E; águila barbuda SAV; águila L; águila chivata E; barbudo C^3; osífraga, osífrago EV; franhueso ACo; frangüeso Co.

FALCONIDAE

111. Aquila chrysaëtos (Golden eagle): águila real SEJLlAVB; águila negra IC^{3}VeE; águila dorada EJ; águila chivera LlJ^2; águila de las rocas Ve; águila caudal, águila caudalosa AV; águila común E.

112. Aquila heliaca (Imperial eagle): águila imperial SEJLlAVB; águila real LIVe; águila negra, águila de los árboles Ve.

113. Aquila rapax (Tawny eagle): águila rapaz BJ^2.

114. Aquila clanga (Spotted eagle): águila moteada BJ^2; águila maculada J^2; águila chillona mayor E.

115. Aquila nipalensis (Steppe-eagle): águila nipalense, águila de estepa J^2; águila de las estepas E.

116. Aquila pomarina (Lesser spotted eagle): águila pomerana BJ^2; águila manchada EJ^1; águila chillona E.

117. Hieraëtus fasciatus (Bonelli's eagle): águila perdicera SC^{2}IC^{3}EJB; águila perdiguera LlA; perdicero L; águila liebrera EJ; águila blancuzca S; águila blanca L; águila pintada C^4; águila de las rocas I; águila acciptrina, águila de Bonelli E.

118. Hieraëtus pennatus (Booted eagle): águila calzada SEJLlAVB; águila blanca L; águila enana, águila conejera E; águila bastarda EAV; aguilucho SEV; /azor/E.

119. Buteo buteo (Buzzard): ratonero común BJ^2; águila ratonera J^1D; águila ratera EAJ^2; aguililla ratonera $LlAJ^2$; arpella I; pella S; meleón E; mileón (melión?) LlJ^2; busardo, buso, buzo ED; buzo común J; /alfaneque/V.

119a. B. b. vulpinus (Desert-buzzard): ratonero rubio BJ^2.

120. Buteo lagopus (Rough-legged buzzard): ratonero calzado B^2J^2; buzo patudo J.

121. Buteo rufinus (Long-legged buzzard): ratonero moro B^2J^2.

122. Accipiter nisus (Sparrow-hawk): gavilán $LSIC^3EJ^1LlAVB$; gavilán común EDJ^2; gavilán de los gorriones D; milano jaspeado I; vilano V; esparver SE; esparvel, accípiter, accípitre, niso común E; galfarro A; /cernícalo/S; /primilla/E.

123. Accipiter brevipes (Levant sparrow-hawk): gavilán griego B^2J^2.

124. Accipiter gentilis (Goshawk): azor LSIEJLl?AVB; azor de las zuritas EJ; águila gallinera J; gavilán SI; gavilán de las palomas ED; halcón palumbario, ferre ?A; /milano/AV; /esmerejón/V.

125. Milvus milvus (Kite): milano real $LSIC^3JLlDB$; milano rojo D; milano EV; vilano A.

126. Milvus migrans (Black kite): milano negro LSIEJLlB.

127. Elanus caeruleus (Black-winged kite): elanio azul BJ^2; elano ?E.

128. Haliaëtus albicilla (White-tailed eagle): pigargo común JB^1; pigargo $E?VDB^2$; águila marina LlJ^2; águila marina grande ED; águila leona C^3; águila pescadora E; melión V; quebrantahuesos ED.

129. Haliaëtus leucoryphus (Pallas's sea-eagle): pigargo de Pallas B^2J^2; pigargo cabeciblanco J^2; águila de cabeza blanca J; quebrantahuesos de cabeza blanca E.

130. Pernis apivorus (Honey-buzzard): halcón abejero $ELlBJ^2$; águila de moros I; pilotero S; /friorque/(triorque) apívoro J^1; /gavilán/S.

131. Circus aeruginosus (Marsh-harrier): aguilucho lagunero BJ^2; aguilucho I; águila de ribera LlJ^2; arpella LSJLl?AVD; busardo E; halcón coronado ?A; milano S; /borní/EV; /rapiña/I.

132. Circus cyaneus (Hen-harrier): aguilucho pálido BJ^2; cenizo SIELl; milano gris J^1; milano blanco LE; ave de San Martín $IELlJ^2$; buzardo azulado J; busardo E.

133. Circus macrourus (Pallid harrier): aguilucho papialbo BJ^2; buzardo pálido J; busardo E.

134. Circus pygargus (Montagu's harrier): aguilucho cenizo BJ^2; cenizo SIELl; buzardo ceniciento J; busardo E.

135. Circaëtus gallicus (Short-toed eagle): águila culebrera ELlABJ^2; culebrera I; águila serpentaria E; serpentario J^1; águila melión S; melión I; águila parda IA; circaeto J^1; atahorma V.

136. Pandion haliaëtus (Osprey): águila pescadora SIC^{3}EJAB; aguililla pescadora Ll; águila blanca, águila de río E; halieto, aleto, /pigargo/, /quebrantahuesos/V.

137. Falco subbuteo (Hobby): alcotán SIEJLlVB; bigotudo E; /buaro/J^1.

138. Falco peregrinus (Peregrine): halcón común EBJ^2; halcón LSI Ll?AV; halcón real EJ; halcón peregrino ED; halcón neblí J^2; neblí EJLl?A; halcón gentil E?A.

    138a. F. p. peregrinus (Peregrine): halcón neblí B^1; neblí EJLlA.

    138b. F. p. brookei (Mediterranean falcon): halcón baharí B^1; baharí, /tagarote/?V.

    138c. F. p. pelegrinoides (Barbary falcon): halcón tagarote B^1; tagarote, /baharí/?V.

139. Falco biarmicus (Lanner falcon): halcón borní BJ^2; borní ?A; halcón lanario J?A; alfaneque Ll?AJ^2.

140. Falco cherrug (Saker falcon): halcón sacre B^{2}J^2.

141. Falco rusticolus (Gyr falcon): halcón gerifalte BJ^2; gerifalte EJV; gerifalco E.

142. Falco eleonorae (Eleonora's falcon): halcón de Eleonor B^{2}J^2; halcón de /eleonor/B^1.

143. Falco columbarius (Merlin): esmerejón LIC^{3}EJLlDB; alcotán palomero E; /tagarote/E.

144. Falco vespertinus (Red-footed falcon): cernícalo patirrojo BJ^2; halcón vespertino J.

145. Falco naumanni (Lesser kestrel): cernícalo primilla BJ^2; primilla LSIC^{3}EJLl; primita J; /buaro/L.

146. Falco tinnunculus (Kestrel): cernícalo vulgar BJ^2; cernícalo común J^1; cernícalo LSIELlV; mochete EV; tinúnculo E; /primilla/SE; /alfaneque/, /alfaneto/, /sacre/E.

147. Falco sparverius (American sparrow-hawk): cernícalo yanqui B^{2}J^2.

GALLIFORMES

TETRAONIDAE

148. **Lagopus lagopus** (Willow-grouse): lagópodo escandinavo B^2J^2; perdiz patiblanca, patiblanca E?A; perdiz blancal ?A.
149. **Lagopus scoticus** (Red grouse): lagópodo escocés B^2J^2.
150. **Lagopus mutus** (Ptarmigan): perdiz nival BJ^2; perdiz blanca EJLlAV; /ptarmigan/J^2.
151. **Lyrurus tetrix** (Black grouse): gallo lira B^2J^2; pequeño gallo de bosque J; grigallo D; gallina silvestre E; /cua furxada/E.
152. **Tetrao urogallus** (Capercaillie): urogallo $EPVDBJ^2$; gallo de bosque LEJ; gallo de monte LlJ^2; gallo montés D; /grigallo/V; gallo silvestre ED; faisán IELl; faisán cantábrico J^2; tetrao común E.
153. **Tetrastes bonasia** (Hazel-hen): grévol BJ^2; grébul J^2; grebul J^1; gallina montés SoJ^2; bonasa ED.

PHASIANIDAE

154. **Alectoris graeca** (Rock-partridge): perdiz griega JB^2; perdiz de las rocas EJ.
155. **Alectoris barbara** (Barbary partridge): perdiz moruna BJ^2; perdiz mora LlJ^2.
156. **Alectoris rufa** (Red-legged partridge): perdiz común BJ^2; perdiz SIJ^1LlAV; perdiz roja EJLlV; perdiz real AV.
157. **Francolinus francolinus** (Francolin): francolín de collar J^2; francolín común E.
158. **Perdix perdix** (Partridge): perdiz pardilla $EAVBJ^2$; pardilla J; pardillo A; perdiz LlD; perdiz gris EJ; perdiz cenicienta, estarno E; estarna EV; charra J^2.
159. **Coturnix coturnix** (Quail): codorniz $LSIC^3EJLlAPVDB$; pazpallá J^2.
  159a. **C. c. coturnix** (Quail): codorniz común B^1.
  159b. **C. c. confisa** (Madeiran quail): codorniz canaria B^1.
160. **Phasianus colchicus** (Pheasant): faisán vulgar BJ^2; faisán común EJ^1D; faisán de collar blanco E; faisán chino de collar Le; faisán LlAV.

RALLIFORMES

TURNICIDAE

161. Turnix sylvatica (Andalusian button-quail): torillo SC^{1}IC^{3}JLlAB.

BALEARICIDAE

162. Megalornis grus (Crane): grulla común EBJ^2; grulla SIC^{3}EJ^1 LlAPV; grulla cenicienta EJ; grulla real, grulla coronada ?E; grúa EA.
163. Megalornis leucogeranus (Asiatic white crane): grulla siberiana blanca B^2; grulla blanca EJ^2.
164. Anthropoides virgo (Demoiselle crane): grulla damisela BJ^2; grulla moruna SIJ; grulla mora LlJ^2; grulla de Numidia EJ; grulla coronada ?E.

RALLIDAE

165. Rallus aquaticus (Water-rail): rascón SIELlBJ^2; rascón de agua IJLl; polluela I; mataperros C^3; ralo acuático E.
166. Porzana porzana (Spotted crake): polluela pintoja BJ^2; polluela común J^1; polluela I; pollo de agua S; polla de agua porzana J^1; mataperros C^3.
167. Porzana pusilla (Baillon's crake): polluela chica JB; polluela I; pollo de agua S; polla de agua Baillon J; mataperros C^3.
168. Porzana parva (Little crake): polluela bastarda BJ^2; polluela pequeña J^1; polluela I; pollo de agua S; mataperros C^3.
169. Porzana carolina (Sora rail, Carolina crake): polluela de la Carolina B^{2}J^2.
170. Crex crex (Corncrake): guión de codornices SEABJ^2; guión de las codornices ELl; guía de las codornices I; rey de las codornices ILlJ^2; rey de codornices EAV; polluela rubia I; rascón de los prados EJ; rascón de retama J; rascón E; mataperros C^3; bitor APV; /polla de agua/EV.
171. Porphyrio porphyrio (Purple gallinule): calamón común BJ^2; calamón SIELlVJ^2; mancón azul I; gallo azul S^{1}S; gallo de cañar J^2; gallo de /Cañar/S.

172. Porphyrio madagascariensis (Green-backed gallinule): calamón dorsiverde B^2J^2.

173. Porphyrula alleni (Allen's gallinule): calamón de Allen BJ^2.

174. Gallinula chloropus (Moorhen): polla de agua SIEJLlB; polla V; gallina de río E; florentina LlJ^2.

175. Fulica atra (Coot): focha común JB; focha SELlVDJ^2; foja EVD; fúlica negra ED; fúlica E; mancón SI; gallareta IELlVJ^2; gallineta E; gallina de agua EJ; falaris, pájaro diablo EV; polla de agua E; /rascón/, /ralo acuático/D.

176. Fulica cristata (Crested coot): focha cornuda BJ^2; gallareta IEJ^1; gallareta cornuda J^2.

OTIDIDAE

177. Otis tarda (Great bustard): avutarda LSIC^{2}C^{3}ELlAPVBJ^2; abutarda ELlJ^2; avutarda mayor EJ^1; avetarda EV; avucasta EAV; avucastro V; gallarón, oto E.

178. Otis tetrax (Little bustard): sisón LSC^{2}IC^{3}VeREJAVB; avutarda menor EJ^1A; /gallarón/V; /francolino/I.

179. Chlamydotis undulata (Houbara bustard): hubara BJ^2.
179a. C. u. undulata (Houbara bustard): hubara mora B^1.
179b. C. u. fuerteventurae (—): hubara canaria B^1.

CHARADRIIFORMES

HAEMATOPODIDAE

180. Haematopus ostralegus (Oystercatcher): ostrero IEJLlB; zampa-ostras J^1; zampaostras J^2; vuelvepiedras S; garza de mar, hematópodo E.
180a. H. o. ostralegus (Oystercatcher): ostrero común B^1.
180b. H. o. meadewaldoi (Black oystercatcher): ostrero unicolor B^1.

CHARADRIIDAE

181. Chettusia leucura (White-tailed plover): chorlito coliblanco B^2J^2

182. Chettusia gregaria (Sociable plover): chorlito social BJ^2.

183. Vanellus vanellus (Lapwing); avefría $PVDBJ^2$; ave fría $SIEJ^1$ LlAV; judía $SIEJ^2$; aguanieves LlJ^2; nevera J^2; quinceta J^2; quincineta V; frailecillo VD; vanelo E.

184. Hoplopterus spinosus (Spur-winged plover): avefría espolada B^2J^2; tero EAP; teruteru EA; terutero EP; güerequeque ?EP; huerequeque ?E.

185. Charadrius hiaticula (Ringed plover): chorlitejo grande BJ^2; chorlito de collar J; andarríos SIJ; correrríos I; correplaya S; frailecillo I.

186. Charadrius dubius (Little ringed plover): chorlitejo chico BJ^2; andarríos pequeño, pluvial pequeño J.

187. Charadrius alexandrinus (Kentish plover): chorlitejo patinegro BJ^2; andarríos $ILlJ^2$; andarrío E; andarríos de Kent J; charrán ILl; frailecillo S; pluvial de collar interrumpido J.

188. Charadrius vociferus (Killdeer): chorlitejo culirrojo B^2J^2.

189. Charadrius asiaticus (Caspian plover): chorlitejo asiático B^2J^2.

190. Charadrius leschenaultii (Greater sand-plover): chorlitejo mongol B^2J^2.

191. Charadrius squatarola (Grey plover): chorlito gris BJ^2; chorlito SE; redolín $ILlJ^2$; pluvial gris J; ave fría vistosa J^1; escuatarola E.

192. Charadrius apricarius (Golden plover): chorlito dorado común BJ^2; chorlito dorado J^1; chorlito SIELlV; pluvial dorado EJ; pildoré, francolín pequeño E.

193. Charadrius dominicus (American golden plover): chorlito dorado chico BJ^2.

    193a. C. d. dominicus (American golden plover): chorlito dorado chico J^2.

    193b. C. d. fulvus (Asiatic golden plover): chorlito siberiano J^2.

194. Charadrius morinellus (Dotterel): chorlito carambolo BJ^2; carambolo sereño LlJ^2; chorlito marismeño S; medio chorlito J^1; morinelo EJ.

195. Arenaria interpres (Turnstone): vuelvepiedras SBJ^2; revuelvepiedras IEJLlAPV; pillera LlJ^2.

SCOLOPACIDAE

196. Capella gallinago (Common snipe): agachadiza común EJB; agachadiza SIC^3LlVJ^2; agachadera SI; agachona IC^3VLe; gacha J^2; rayuelo V; sorda EV; arciucha, becacica J^2; becacina, becacina mediana E; /chocha/, /becada/, /picuda/D.

197. Capella media (Great snipe): agachadiza real $ILlBJ^2$; agachadiza grande J; agachadiza mayor, agachadiza doble, becacina grande E.

198. Lymnocryptes minimus (Jack-snipe): agachadiza chica BJ^2; agachadiza pequeña J; agachadiza menor E; agachadiza sorda J^1; agachadiza SLl; agachadera S; gacha menor J^2; becacina pequeña E.

199. Scolopax rusticola (Woodcock): chocha perdiz $LlBJ^2$; chochaperdiz EV; perdiz chocha J^1; chocha $SIC^3ELlAPV$; chorcha EV; gallineta SIC^3VJ^2; gallineta ciega E; gallina sorda EAV; sorda EJ^2; becada común J^1; becada $EAPVJ^2$; pitorra $EAVJ^2$; coalla EV; arcea J^2.

200. Bartramia longicauda (Upland sandpiper): correlimos de Bartram B^2J^2.

201. Numenius arquatus (Curlew): zarapito real SEJB; zarapito ILl $?VJ^2$; sarapico ?V; culisca, alcaraván E.

202. Numenius phaeopus (Whimbrel): zarapito trinador BJ^2; zarapito común J^1; zarapito SE; zarapito de casquete J.
202a. N. p. phaeopus (Whimbrel): zarapito trinador común B^1.
202b. N. p. hudsonicus (Hudsonian curlew): zarapito trinador hudsónico B^1.

203. Numenius borealis (Eskimo curlew): zarapito esquimal B^2J^2.

204. Numenius tenuirostris (Slender-billed curlew): zarapito fino BJ^2; zarapito menor J; zarapito de pico fino J^1; zarapito de pico delgado J^2; zarapito S.

205. Limosa limosa (Black-tailed godwit): aguja colinegra BJ^2; agujeta J^1; abujeta $ILlJ^2$; abuja LlJ^2; sarseruelo I; limosa egocéfala J^1.

206. Limosa lapponica (Bar-tailed godwit): aguja colipinta BJ^2; limosa roja J.

207. Tringa ochropus (Green sandpiper): andarríos grande BJ^2; lavandera $ILlJ^2$; caballero culo blanco, arenosa, tótano de los ríos J^1; totano verde E.

208. Tringa glareola (Wood-sandpiper): andarríos bastardo BJ²; caballero silvestre J¹; caballero silvícola J²; valona E; /carregadet/J¹.

209. Tringa solitaria (Solitary sandpiper): andarríos solitario B²J²; totano solitario E.

210. Tringa hypoleuca (Common sandpiper): andarríos chico BJ²; andarríos Ll; lavandera chica IJ; lavandera común J; lavandera E.

211. Tringa macularia (Spotted sandpiper): andarríos maculado B²J².

212. Tringa totanus (Redshank): archibebe común BJ²; archibebe ILlJ²; totano de patas rojas E; caballero/gambetta/J.

213. Tringa erythropus (Spotted redshank): archibebe oscuro BJ²; caballero pardo J¹.

214. Tringa melanoleuca (Greater yellowlegs): archibebe patigualdo grande B²J²; totano grande E.

215. Tringa flavipes (Lesser yellowlegs): archibebe patigualdo chico B²J².

216. Tringa nebularia (Greenshank): archibebe claro BJ²; caballero gris J.

217. Tringa stagnatilis (Marsh-sandpiper): archibebe fino BJ²; caballero de los estanques, chorlito J¹.

218. Tringa brevipes (Grey-rumped sandpiper): archibebe paticorto B²J².

219. Xenus cinerea (Terek sandpiper): andarríos /de/(del) Terek BJ².

220. Limnodromus griseus (Dowitcher): agujeta gris B²J².

221. Calidris canutus (Knot): correlimos gordo BJ²; tringa gris J¹; canut EJ.

222. Calidris maritima (Purple sandpiper): correlimos oscuro BJ²; churrilla J; arenatela E.

223. Calidris minuta (Little stint): correlimos menudo BJ²; churrilla minuta J; churlita E; pelidna enana J¹.

224. Calidris minutilla (Least sandpiper, American stint): correlimos menudillo B²J².

225. Calidris temminckii (Temminck's stint): correlimos de Temminck BJ²; pelidna de Temminck J¹; terrerita J.

226. Calidris fuscicollis (White-rumped sandpiper, Bonaparte's sandpiper): correlimos de Bonaparte B²J².

227. Calidris bairdii (Baird's sandpiper): correlimos de Baird B²J².

228. Calidris acuminata (Siberian pectoral sandpiper): correlimos acuminado B²J².

229. Calidris melanotos (Pectoral sandpiper): correlimos pectoral B²J².

230. Calidris alpina (Dunlin): correlimos común BJ²; pelidna de los Alpes J¹; churra J²; mondra de mar, pío LlJ².

231. Calidris testacea (Curlew-sandpiper): correlimos zarapitín BJ²; pelidna cocorlí J¹; pitillo Ll.

232. Calidris pusilla (Semi-palmated sandpiper): correlimos semipalmeado B²J².

233. Crocethia alba (Sanderling): correlimos tridáctilo BJ²; churrilla de tres dedos I; churrilla LlJ²; calidris de los arenales J¹; /sanderling/P.

234. Limicola falcinellus (Broad-billed sandpiper): correlimos falcinelo BJ²; limicola pigmeo J¹.

235. Tryngites subruficollis (Buff-breasted sandpiper): correlimos canelo B²J².

236. Philomachus pugnax (Ruff): combatiente SEBJ²; combatiente común J¹; maquetes E.

RECURVIROSTRIDAE

237. Recurvirostra avosetta (Avocet): avoceta IJLlAPVB; avoceta común E; boceta S; vaqueruela, baquiñuela J².

238. Himantopus himantopus (Black-winged stilt): cigüeñuela ELlA BJ²; cigüenela I; cigüiñuela E; ciguiñuela J¹; cinguinela S; cigoñuela D; zancas largas J; zancolín J²; zancudo común ED; zancuda P; /rabilargo/Ll.

PHALAROPODIDAE

239. Phalaropus fulicarius (Grey phalarope): falaropo picogrueso BJ²; falarópodo J¹; falarópodo gris E.

240. Phalaropus lobatus (Red-necked phalarope): falaropo picofino BJ²; falaropo rojo J¹; falarópodo de cuello rojo E.

BURHINIDAE

241. Burhinus oedicnemus (Stone-curlew): alcaraván LSIJLlVB; alcaraván común E; chorlito LlJ²; dormitón J²; /árdea/, /charadrio/V.

GLAREOLIDAE

242. Pluvianus aegyptius (Crocodile plover): pluvial egipcio BJ^2.
243. Glareola pratincola (Collared pratincole): canastera SEJLlB; canastela I; perdiz de mar EJLl; perdiz de las arenas J; carregadora E.
244. Glareola nordmanni (Black-winged pratincole): canastera alinegra B^2J^2; glareola de alas negras E.
245. Cursorius cursor (Cream-coloured courser): corredor EBJ^2; corredor de Europa, corredor isabela J; engañamuchachos LlJ^2.

STERCORARIIDAE

246. Stercorarius parasiticus (Arctic skua): págalo parasítico B; págalo parásito J^2; cágalo SIE; estercorario EJ^1; estercolero E; estercorario/de cola larga/J^2.
247. Stercorarius skua (Great skua): págalo grande BJ^2; cágalo SE; salteador, /skua/J; estercorario EJ^2.
248. Stercorarius pomarinus (Pomatorhine skua): págalo pomarino BJ^2; cágalo SE; estercorario EJ; salteador, /skua/J^2.
249. Stercorarius longicaudus (Long-tailed skua): págalo rabero BJ^2; cágalo SE; estercorario de cola larga J.

LARIDAE

250. Pagophila eburnea (Ivory gull): gaviota marfil B^2J^2.
251. Larus marinus (Greater black-backed gull): gavión BJ^2; gaviota gigante J; gaviota marina E.
252. Larus fuscus (Lesser black-backed gull): gaviota sombría BJ^2; gaviota oscura J; gaviota negra E; gaviota de pies amarillos J^1.
253. Larus argentatus (Herring-gull): gaviota argéntea BJ^2; gaviota común EJ^1; gaviota, paviota EV.
254. Larus canus (Common gull): gaviota cana BJ^2; gaviota blanca EJ; /gavinot/J.
255. Larus hyperboreus (Glaucous gull): gaviota hiperbórea BJ^2; gaviota J^1.
256. Larus glaucoides (Iceland gull): gaviota polar BJ^2.

257. Larus ichthyaëtus (Great black-headed gull): gavión cabecinegro B²J²; gaviota turca J².

258. Larus audouinii (Audouin's gull): gaviota de Audouin BJ²; gaviota J¹.

259. Larus genei (Slender-billed gull): gaviota picofina BJ²; gaviota J¹.

260. Larus philadelphia (Bonaparte's gull): gaviota de Bonaparte B²J²

261. Larus melanocephalus (Mediterranean black-headed gull): gaviota cabecinegra BJ²; gaviota de cabeza negra EJ.

262. Larus minutus (Little gull): gaviota enana BJ².

263. Larus ridibundus (Black-headed gull): gaviota reidora común B; gaviota reidora, gaviota común J²; gaviota de cabeza negra EJ¹D; /laro ridibundo/D.

264. Rhodostethia rosea (Ross's gull): gaviota de Ross B²J²; gaviota rosa E.

265. Xema sabini (Sabine's gull): gaviota de Sabine BJ².

266. Rissa tridactyla (Kittiwake): gaviota tridáctila BJ²; gaviota de tres dedos J; gavina Ll.

267. Chlidonias niger (Black tern): fumarel común BJ²; cencerrillo ILlJ²; paino (paíño?) I; /picotijera/J¹.

268. Chlidonias leucopterus (White-winged black tern): fumarel aliblanco BJ²; golondrina de mar J.

269. Chlidonias hybridus (Whiskered tern): fumarel cariblanco BJ²; golondrina de mar J¹; paino (paíño?) mayor ILlJ².

270. Gelochelidon nilotica (Gull-billed tern): pagaza piconegra BJ²; golondrina de mar J¹; cágalo ILl.

271. Hydroprogne caspia (Caspian tern): pagaza piquirroja BJ²; golondrina de mar I.

272. Sterna hirundo (Common tern): charrán común BJ²; gran golondrina de mar J¹; golondrina de mar común E.

273. Sterna paradisea (Arctic tern): charrán ártico BJ²; golondrina de mar ártica E; gavina J¹.

274. Sterna dougallii (Roseate tern): charrán rosado BJ²; /carrán/ (charrán) de Dougall J²; golondrina de mar rosácea E.

275. Sterna fuscata (Sooty tern): charrán sombrío B²J²; gaviota monja J¹.

276. Sterna anaethetus (Bridled tern): charrán embridado B²J².

277. Sterna albifrons (Little tern): charrancito BJ²; catalinita IJLl; golondrina de mar chica J; golondrina de mar enana E?D.

278. Sterna maxima (Royal tern): charrán gigante B¹.

279. Sterna sandvicensis (Sandwich tern): charrán patinegro BJ^2; charrán $IL1J^2$; golondrina de mar moñuda J; golondrina de mar gigante E.

280. Sterna bengalensis (Lesser crested tern): charrán bengalés BJ^2.

281. Anous stolidus (Noddy): charrán pardelo B^2J^2.

ALCIDAE

282. Alca torda (Razorbill): alca común BJ^2; gallareta de mar IJ; gallo Ll; pingüino EJLl; carolo LlJ^2; potorra, potorro E.

*283. Pinguinis impennis (Great auk): alca gigante, pingüino gigante J^2; pingüino E.

284. Plautus alle (Little auk): mérgulo marino BJ^2; mérgulo EJ^1; alca enana J.

285. Uria aalge (Guillemot): arao común BJ^2; arau J^1; arán LlJ^2; aro, pitorro J^2; uría común ED; pingüino E.

286. Uria lomvia (Brünnich's guillemot): arao de Brünnich BJ^2; uria J; guillemote J^1; uría lomvia, pingüino E.

287. Uria grylle (Black guillemot): arao aliblanco B^2J^2; uría de alas blancas, pingüino E.

288. Cyclorrhynchus psittacula (Paroquet auklet): mérgulo lorito B^2J^2.

289. Aethia cristatella (Crested auklet): mérgulo crestado B^2J^2.

290. Fratercula arctica (Puffin): frailecillo común BJ^2; frailecillo IEJLl; gallo de mar J^2; mormón E.

COLUMBIFORMES

PTEROCLIDAE

291. Pterocles orientalis (Black-bellied sand-grouse): ortega LSEJLlA PVB; corteza $SC^1IC^3LlVJ^2$; churra $LSLlVJ^2$; turra LlJ^2; /xurra/E.

292. Pterocles alchata (Pin-tailed sand-grouse): ganga común BJ^2; ganga $LSC^1C^2IC^3EJLlAPV$.

293. Pterocles senegallus (Spotted sand-grouse): ganga moteada B^2J^2.

294. Syrrhaptes paradoxus (Pallas's sand-grouse): ganga de Pallas BJ^2; ganga del desierto J.

COLUMBIDAE

295. Columba oenas (Stock-dove): paloma zurita JAB; zurita LlJ²; paloma zorita, paloma zura, paloma zurana A; paloma brava EJV; paloma silvestre EV.

286. Columba livia (Rock-dove): paloma bravía BJ²; paloma brava SIA; paloma silvestre LlAJ²; paloma montés J; paloma roquiza E; zurita IE; paloma zurita V; paloma zurana JV; paloma zurra V; zura E.

297. Columba palumbus (Wood-pigeon): paloma torcaz SIEJLlAVB; torcazo, torcaza V; paloma silvestre J; paloma de collar E.

298. Columba trocaz (Madeiran pigeon): paloma turque B¹.

299. Columba junoniae (Canarian laurel-pigeon): paloma rabiche B¹.

300. Streptopelia turtur (Turtle-dove): tórtola común EBJ²; tórtola SIJ¹LlAPVD; rolla A.

301. Streptopelia decaocto (Collared turtle-dove): tórtola turca B²J²; tórtola de collar J¹.

302. Streptopelia orientalis (Rufous turtle-dove): tórtola oriental B²J²

CUCULIFORMES

CUCULIDAE

303. Cuculus canorus (Cuckoo): cuco IELlADBJ²; cucu S; cuclillo común EJ¹D; cuclillo ELlAVJ²; cuclillo de Europa, cuquillo E.

304. Clamator glandarius (Great spotted cuckoo): críalo BJ²; cuco real IJLlA56; cucu real S; cuclillo real E; cuco moñón ILlAJ²; cucu del moño S; carrión J².

305. Coccyzus erythrophthalmus (Black-billed cuckoo): cuco piquinegro B²J².

306. Coccyzus americanus (Yellow-billed cuckoo): cuco piquigualdo B²J².

STRIGIFORMES

STRIGIDAE

307. Tyto alba (Barn-owl): lechuza común EJB; lechuza LSIC^{3}E LlAPCoVDJ^2; curuja EAVJ^2; coruja VJ^2; curuca EV; bruja EJA CoV; /estrige/, /oliva/EAV; /cárabo/Co.

308. Otus scops (Scops owl): autillo BJ^2; corneja LIEJLlAV; corneta SI; cornichuela J; cucu S; cuquillo I; coruja Ll; buho pequeño J^1; buharro, buaro EAV; buarillo E.

309. Bubo bubo (Eagle-owl): buho real EJB; bujo real I; buho grande LS; buho ElICoVDJ^2; bujo E; bújaro LlJ^2; gran duque J?V.

310. Nyctea scandiaca (Snowy owl): buho nival B^{2}J^2; lechuza serval E; harfango de las nieves EJ^1; harfango, nictea alba E.

311. Surnia ulula (Hawk-owl): lechuza gavilana B^{2}J^2; surnio gavilán J^1; surnia ulula, /cárabo/E.

312. Glaucidium passerinum (Pygmy owl): mochuelo chico B^{2}J^2; mochuelo EJ^1; lechuza enana J.

313. Athene noctua (Little owl): mochuelo común BJ^2; mochuelo vulgar J^1; mochuelo LSIELlACoD.

314. Strix aluco (Tawny owl): cárabo LIEJLlAVB^1; cárabo común B^2; autillo, úlula, zumaya, zumacaya EAV; alucón A; /oto/EV; /engañapastor/, /xibeca/E.

315. Strix nebulosa (Great grey owl): cárabo lapón B^{2}J^2.

316. Strix uralensis (Ural owl): cárabo uralense B^{2}J^2.

317. Asio otus (Long-eared owl): buho chico BJ^2; buho pequeño LlJ^2; buho mediano J; buho común J^1; buho de orejas largas D; buho A; bujo C^3; cárabo LSI; /autillo/E.

318. Asio flammeus (Short-eared owl): lechuza campestre JB; lechuza de monte LlJ^2; lechuza de las peñas J^1; cárabo LSIC^3; miloca ?A.

319. Asio capensis (African marsh-owl): lechuza mora BJ^2.

320. Aegolius funereus (Tengmalm's owl): lechuza de Tengmalm BJ^2; mochuelo de Tengmalm J; miloca V.

CAPRIMULGIFORMES

CAPRIMULGIDAE

321. Caprimulgus europaeus (Nightjar): chotacabras gris BJ^2; chotacabras EJ^1APV; papavientos EJ; engañabobos J^2; engañapastores EVJ^2; gallina ciega J^2; pitaciega E; zumaya $EAVJ^2$; /denoiteira/J^2.

322. Caprimulgus ruficollis (Red-necked nightjar): chotacabras pardo BJ^2; chotacabras de collar rojo J; chotacabras SILIAV; papavientos J^2; engañapastores $SILIVJ^2$; engañabobos LIJ^2; zumaya $SIVJ^2$; capacho, gallina ciega LIJ^2; pagañera, /denoiteira/J^2.

323. Caprimulgus aegyptius (Egyptian nightjar): chotacabras egipcio B^2J^2.

324. Chordeiles minor (Common nighthawk, American nighthawk): chotacabras yanqui B^2J^2.

APODIFORMES

APODIDAE

325. Apus apus (Swift): vencejo común EJB; vencejo ELIAPVD; oncejo EV; avión SIJ^2; arrejaco VD; arrejaque D.

326. Apus pallidus (Pallid swift): vencejo pálido BJ^2; avión J^1?A?P.

327. Apus melba (Alpine swift): vencejo real BJ^2; vencejo alpino EJ; vencejo E; avión real IJ; avión de pecho blanco I; avión S; martinete E.

328. Apus affinis (White-rumped swift): vencejo culiblanco B^2J^2.

329. Apus unicolor (Plain swift): vencejo unicolor B^1.

330. Chaetura caudacuta (Needle-tailed swift): rabitojo B^2J^2.

CORACIIFORMES

ALCEDINIDAE

331. Ceryle rudis (Pied kingfisher): martín pescador pío B^2J^2.
332. Ceryle alcyon (Belted kingfisher): martín pescador alción B^2J^2.
333. Alcedo atthis (Kingfisher): martín pescador $SIC^3EJLlAPVDB$; martín cazador, martín zambullidor E; azulillo, azulejo LlJ^2; andarríos Ll; guardarrío, pájaro polilla EV; alción EAPV; alcedón ACo; camaronero E.

MEROPIDAE

334. Merops apiaster (Bee-eater): abejaruco común BJ^2; abejaruco IEJLlAPVD; abejero EAV; canario Ll; azulejo EV.
335. Merops superciliosus (Blue-cheeked bee-eater): abejaruco papirrojo BJ^2; abejaruco bigotudo E.

CORACIIDAE

336. Coracias garrulus (Roller): carraca IEJLlA56B; carlanco SI; carranco S; azulejo $ELlDJ^2$.

UPUPIDAE

337. Upupa epops (Hoopoe): abubilla SIJLlAVB; abubilla común ED; sabubilla I; bubillo LlJ^2; upupa EVD; bupupa Co; gallo de marzo I; gallito marzo J^2; cajonera I; cuquillo LlJ^2.

PICIFORMES

PICIDAE

338. Picus viridis (Green woodpecker): pito real LSIELIVBJ^2; pico real J^1; pico verde EJLIAPV; picorro J^2; pico E; potrilla, potrito LlJ^2; pico carpintero EJ^2; carpintero S?V; pájaro carpintero EV; pitobarrenos J^2; pico barreno EV; pitorrelincho J^2; picarrelincho, picamaderos, picaposte V; herrero E.

339. Picus canus (Grey-headed woodpecker): pito cano B^{2}J^2; pico ceniciento J.

340. Dendrocopos major (Greater spotted woodpecker): pico picapinos BJ^2; picapinos EJ; picapuertas mayor J^2; picapotros E; pico mayor J; pico alazán, pico carpintero LlJ^2; pito real I; picamaderos E.

341. Dendrocopos syriacus (Syrian woodpecker): pico sirio B^{2}J^2.

342. Dendrocopos leucotos (White-backed woodpecker): pico dorsiblanco BJ^2; picapuertas dorsiblanco J^2; pico leuconoto J^1.

343. Dendrocopos minor (Lesser spotted woodpecker): pico menor JLlB; picapuertas menor J^2; picapuerco, picatocino E; pipo EJ; agateador Ll.

344. Dendrocopos medius (Middle spotted woodpecker): pico mediano BJ^2; picapuerco J^1?A?P.

345. Picoides tridactylus (Three-toed woodpecker): pico tridáctilo B^{2}J^2; picoideo tridáctilo J^1.

346. Dryocopus martius (Black woodpecker): pito negro BJ^2; pico negro EJ^{1}Ll; pico carpintero negro E.

347. Jynx torquilla (Wryneck): torcecuello SIC^{3}EJLIAPVB; hormiguero SIEJLIAP; chimbo hormiguero E; lililo I.

PASSERIFORMES

HIRUNDINIDAE

348. Riparia riparia (Sand-martin): avión zapador BJ^2; golondrina de ribera IJoJLl; golondrina de río E; golondrina de San Martín JLl; rebiruelo E.

349. Hirundo rupestris (Crag-martin): avión roquero BJ^2; avión rupestre J^2; golondrina de las rocas J; golondrina silvestre EJ; vencejillo IJoLlJ².

350. Hirundo rustica (Swallow): golondrina común EDBJ²; golondrina SIJoJLlAV; anduriña LlJ²; andorina, andolina, andarina EV; /aureneta/, /oroneta/E.

351. Hirundo daurica (Red-rumped swallow): golondrina dáurica B^2J^2; golondrina daurica B^1; golondrina roja E.

352. Delichon urbica (House-martin): avión común BJ^2; avión ELlV; golondrina de ventana J; golondrina de las ventanas E; golondrina E; vencejo SIJoJ².

ALAUDIDAE

353. Ammomanes deserti (Desert-lark): terrera sahariana B^2J^2.

354. Ammomanes cincturus (Bar-tailed desert-lark): terrera de Franklin B^2; terrera de Francklin J^2.

355. Alaemon alaudipes (Bifasciated lark): alondra ibis B^2J^2.

356. Chersophilus duponti (Dupont's lark): alondra de Dupont BJ^2.

357. Calandrella cinerea (Short-toed lark): terrera común BJ^2; terrera SIJoM; terrerilla SJoMJ; terreruela MJLl; /terreroli/, /tarrarol/, calandreta, churrica, /cotorret/M.

358. Calandrella rufescens (Lesser short-toed lark): terrera marismeña BJ^2; marismeña M; cujaílla I; cajaílla JoM.

359. Melanocorypha calandra (Calandra lark): calandria común EB^2J^2; calandria SIJoMEJLlAVB¹; calandria de los campos M; alondra SIJoMA56; gulloria EV; chirlerona, caladre E.

360. Melanocorypha leucoptera (White-winged lark): calandria aliblanca B^2J^2.

361. Melanocorypha yeltoniensis (Black lark): calandria negra B^2J^2.

362. Eremophila alpestris (Shore-lark): alondra cornuda BJ^2.
    362a. E. a. flava: alondra cornuda lapona B.

363. Eremophila bilopha (Temminck's horned lark): alondra cornuda sahariana B^1.

364. Galerida cristata (Crested lark): cogujada común JB; cogujada MELlAVDJ²; cugujada EV; cogullada M; cujada SJoM; cucua (cucúa?) Jo; carretera IJoM; copetuda J^2; copetuda totovía (totovía copetuda?) J^1; totovía MEAV; tutuvía M; cotovía E; alondra moñuda, carabinera A; correcaminos J^2; tova, copada EV; galerita EVD; cochevís V.

365. Galerida theklae (Thekla lark): cogujada montesina BJ²;
cogujada MLl; cogullada, cujada, totovía, tutuvía M; carretera
IM; /calandria/J¹.

366. Lullula arborea (Wood-lark): totovía MEJDB; cotovía M;
alondra de monte IJoM; alondra de los bosques ED; calandria de
los montes, churra, pitrulín, /llansetina/M.

367. Alauda arvensis (Skylark): alondra común EBJ²; alondra de campo
MJ¹; alondra de los campos E; alondra LlVJ²; alhoja EV;
alova M; /alosa/ME; zurriaga SIJoME; jaracalla Ll;
jacaralla M; terrera IJoMEV; terreruela E; /terrerola/M; caladre
EV; laverca MJ²; copetuda V; chirta E; churra, torrondana,
/titella/, /xirlu/M.

MOTACILLIDAE

368. Anthus novaeseelandiae (Richard's pipit): bisbita de Richard BJ²;
churrica J; cinceta S.

369. Anthus campestris (Tawny pipit): bisbita campestre BJ²; pipí de
los campos, calandrina J; cinceta S.

370. Anthus berthelotii (Berthelot's pipit): bisbita caminero B¹.

371. Anthus trivialis (Tree-pipit): bisbita arbóreo BJ²; bisbita, pit-pit,
pipí EJ¹; alondra pipí J¹; cinceta SJo.

372. Anthus hodgsoni (Indian tree-pipit): bisbita de Hodgson B²J².

373. Anthus gustavi (Pechora pipit): bisbita del Petchora B²J².

374. Anthus pratensis (Meadow-pipit): bisbita común EB; bisbita, pipí,
pipi, pit-pit E; pipí de los prados EJ; alondra de los prados E;
tordilla J; cinceta S; alfarfera E.

375. Anthus cervinus (Red-throated pipit): bisbita gorgirrojo BJ²; pipí
cervino J; cinceta S.

376. Anthus spinoletta (see subspecies): bisbita ribereño B; tordino,
alfarfero J¹.

    376a. A. s. spinoletta (Water-pipit): bisbita ribereño alpino BJ²

    376b. A. s. petrosus (Rock-pipit): bisbita ribereño costero BJ²

    376c. A. s. littoralis (Scandinavian rock-pipit): bisbita ribereño
        costero nórdico J².

377. Motacilla flava (Yellow wagtail): lavandera boyera B; pispita
amarilla SJo; nevadilla IJo.

    377a. M. f. flava (Blue-headed wagtail): lavandera boyera
        alemana B²J².

377b. M. f. beema (Sykes's wagtail): lavandera boyera de Sykes B.

377c. M. f. thunbergi (Grey-headed wagtail): lavandera boyera escandinava BJ^2.

377d. M. f. cinereocapilla (Ashy-headed wagtail): lavandera boyera italiana B.

377e. M. f. iberiae (Spanish wagtail): lavandera boyera ibérica B.

377f. M. f. flavissima (Yellow wagtail): lavandera boyera inglesa BJ^2; lavandera real J^1; nevadilla IJo; pispita Jo.

377g. M. f. feldegg (Black-headed wagtail): lavandera boyera balcánica B^2J^2.

378. Motacilla citreola (Yellow-headed wagtail): lavandera cetrina B^2J^2; nevatilla citrina J.

379. Motacilla cinerea (Grey wagtail): lavandera cascadeña BJ^2; nevatilla gris J; pispita SJo.

380. Motacilla alba (White wagtail): lavandera blanca B.

380a. M. a. alba (White wagtail): lavandera blanca común BJ^2; lavandera $SJoEJ^1LlD$; pispita $SIJoJ^2$; pizpita EVD; pezpita, pizpitillo, pezpítalo EV; pepita J^2; pipita AV; aguzanieves $ELlAPVDJ^2$; aguzanieve E; aguanieves EV; aguanieve E; apuranieves V; pajarita de las nieves Ell $PVDJ^2$; avecilla de las nieves AV; nevereta EV; nevatilla EJAVD; nevatilla de los arroyos blanca E; blanca de los arroyos D; andarríos, caudatrémula EV; rabilarga, rabicandil, culiblanco, culadera E; motolita, motacila EV; chimita, picarrelincho E; golleria LlJ^2; /doradillo/V.

380b. M. a. yarrellii (Pied wagtail): lavandera blanca enlutada BJ^2.

LANIIDAE

381. Lanius collurio (Red-backed shrike): alcaudón dorsirrojo BJ^2; desollador J; godón, /triguero/E.

381a. L. c. isabellinus (Isabelline shrike): alcaudón isabel B^2; alcaudón Isabel J^2.

382. Lanius nubicus (Masked shrike): alcaudón núbico B^2J^2.

383. Lanius senator (Woodchat-shrike): alcaudón común BJ^2; alcaudón menor J; alcaudón $SIJoLlAPV$; caudón EV; gaudón A; galdón, galdona LlJ^2; desollador común J; desollador EAPV; cabezota JLl; pega reborda PV; picaza chillona V; picaza manchada, picagrega, verdugo E?V; chimbo real E.

384. Lanius minor (Lesser grey shrike): alcaudón chico BJ^2; calcidrán real J.
385. Lanius excubitor (Great grey shrike): alcaudón real SIJoJB; alcaudón ELlJ^2; alcaudón picanzo J^2; galdón, pegarrebordas Ll; margaso E.
    385a. L. e. excubitor (Great grey shrike): alcaudón real nórdico B^1.
    385b. L. e. meridionalis (Southern grey shrike): alcaudón real meridional B^1.
    385c. L. e. koenigi (—): alcaudón real moruno B^1.

ORIOLIDAE

386. Oriolus oriolus (Golden oriole): oropéndola LSIC^{3}JoEJLlAPVDB; becafigos LlJ^2; picafigo, papahigo E; papafigo EPV; gálgulo, víreo E; vireo V; /oureol/J^1.

STURNIDAE

387. Sturnus roseus (Rose-coloured starling): estornino rosado EBJ^2; estornino rosa J^1.
388. Sturnus vulgaris (Starling): estornino pinto BJ^2; estornino SIJoEJLlAPV; estornino común ED; picabuey E; tordo LlJ^2; tordo de campanario, tordo de Castilla EA.
389. Sturnus unicolor (Spotless starling): estornino negro EBJ^2; tordo SIJoLlJ^2; tordo serrano EAJ^2; tordo campanero J^2; tordo solitario EJ^2.

CORVIDAE

390. Perisoreus infaustus (Siberian jay): arrendajo funesto B^{2}J^2.
391. Garrulus glandarius (Jay): arrendajo común EDB^2; arrendajo LSIJoEJLlAPVB^1; arrendajo glandívoro E; rendajo EV; rendaja LlJ^2; cabezón SJo; gayo ELlJ^2; glayo A; pega T; pega rebordada J^2; grajo, esquilaso E.
392. Cyanopica cyanus (Azure-winged magpie): rabilargo LSEJLlAPVB; mohino rabilargo IJo; mohino LSIJoLlVJ^2; gálgulo EPV; ruipego L.

393. Pica pica (Magpie): urraca SIJoEJLlAPVDB; aburraca Jo; marica SIEJLlAPVD; marica común E; pega ELlVJ^2; pica rústica E; picaza EJAVD; picaraza, cotorra EV; gaya V; blanca A.

394. Nucifraga caryocatactes (Nutcracker): cascanueces EJA48PVB; nucífraga, nucífraga E.

395. Pyrrhocorax pyrrhocorax (Chough): chova piquirroja BJ^2; chova JLl; graja de pico encarnado J; graja de pico bermejo, graja de pico rojo E; graja SIJo; grajilla LlJ^2; grajo AP.

396. Pyrrhocorax graculus (Alpine chough): chova piquigualda BJ^2; chova piquiamarilla J^2; graja de pico amarillo EJ; /gralha de pico vermelho/E; graja SJo; grajo J^1; cucala S.

397. Corvus monedula (Jackdaw): grajilla EJLlB; graja IJo; graja menor J^2; chova E; corneja de campanario J^1; /corneja blanca/E.

398. Corvus frugilegus (Rook): graja BJ^2; grajo ELlVD; chova EJ^{1}LlVD; corneja calva J; cuervo merendero V.

399. Corvus corone (Crow): corneja B^1.
    399a. C. c. corone (Carrion-crow): corneja negra EJB; corneja A56P; grajillo SJo; grajilla IJo; grajo Ll; graja E; cuervo LlJ^2; chova A56.
    399b. C. c. cornix (Hooded crow): corneja cenicienta EBJ^2; corneja A48; graja cenicienta J^1; chova A48.

400. Corvus corax (Raven): cuervo SIJoEJLlAPVB; grajo SJ.

BOMBYCILLIDAE

401. Bombycilla garrulus (Waxwing): ampelis europeo BJ^2; ampelis E; ampélido J^2; picotero vulgar J^1; picotero de Europa E.

CINCLIDAE

402. Cinclus cinclus (Dipper): mirlo acuático BJ^2; mirlo de agua EJLl; tordo de agua IC^{3}JoEJAPV; pechiblanco IC^{3}Jo; andarríos LlJ^2.

TROGLODYTIDAE

403. Troglodytes troglodytes (Wren): chochín ELlDBJ^2; chochita ED; ratilla SIC^{3}JoED; castañita EJLlD; almendrita Ll; cucito IJo; carniza TLl; carrizo J^2; percha, epecha E; chepecha, coletero, rey de zarza ED; troglodita EJAP; troglodito pequeño, /cargolet/E; /gargolet/ED.

PRUNELLIDAE

404. Prunella collaris (Alpine accentor): acentor alpino BJ^2; acéntor de los Alpes J^1; acentor de los Alpes, alondra de las rocas E; serrano SIJoJ.

405. Prunella montanella (Siberian accentor): acentor de Pallas B^2J^2; acentor de mejillas negras E.

406. Prunella modularis (Hedge-sparrow): acentor común BJ^2; acéntor silvestre J; acentor de bosque E; churruca JoJ^1; /pardal de bardissa/E; /ferreira/T.

MIMIDAE

407. Dumetella carolinensis (Cat-bird): pájaro gato B^2J^2.

MUSCICAPIDAE

Sylviinae

408. Cettia cetti (Cetti's warbler): ruiseñor bastardo BJ^2; picofino J^1.

409. Locustella fasciolata (Gray's grasshopper-warbler): buscarla de Gray B^2J^2.

410. Locustella luscinoides (Savi's warbler): buscarla unicolor BJ^2; locustela de carrizal J^1.

411. Locustella fluviatilis (River-warbler): buscarla fluvial B^2J^2; locustela fluvial J^1.

412. Locustella certhiola (Pallas's grasshopper-warbler): buscarla de Pallas B^2J^2.

413. Locustella naevia (Grasshopper-warbler): buscarla pintoja BJ^2; buscarla pinta J^2; locustela manchada J^1.

414. Locustella lanceolata (Lanceolated warbler): buscarla lanceolada B^2J^2.

415. Lusciniola melanopogon (Moustached warbler): carricerín real BJ^2.

416. Acrocephalus paludicola (Aquatic warbler): carricerín cejudo BJ^2; arandillo J^1V; saltamimbres J^1; trepajuncos V.

417.- Acrocephalus schoenobaenus (Sedge-warbler): carricerín común BJ^2; ruiseñor silvestre J^1; /salta marges/E.

418. Acrocephalus agricola (Paddy-field warbler): carricero agrícola B^2J^2.
419. Acrocephalus dumetorum (Blyth's reed-warbler): carricero de Blyth B^2J^2.
420. Acrocephalus palustris (Marsh-warbler): carricero poliglota B^2J^2; carricero políglota B^1; cañamera J^1.
421. Acrocephalus scirpaceus (Reed-warbler): carricero común BJ^2; pinzoleta JoJ^1; buscarla J^1.
422. Acrocephalus arundinaceus (Great reed-warbler): carricero tordal BJ^2; carrizalero $IJoLlJ^2$; carrisalero SJ^1; carrecera grande Jo; /moscaret/Ll; /tayaret/E.
423. Hippolais icterina (Icterine warbler): zarcero icterino BJ^2; curruca de pecho amarillo J^1.
424. Hippolais polyglotta (Melodious warbler): zarcero común BJ^2; almendrita de verano IJoJ; /carisalero/(carrizalero) S.
425. Hippolais olivetorum (Olive-tree warbler): zarcero grande B^2J^2.
426. Hippolais pallida (Olivaceous warbler): zarcero pálido BJ^2; pinchahigos J^1; viñera Jo.
427. Hippolais caligata (Booted warbler): zarcero escita B^2J^2.
428. Sylvia nisoria (Barred warbler): curruca gavilana B^2J^2; curruca gavilán J^1.
429. Sylvia hortensis (Orphean warbler): curruca mirlona BJ^2; curruca común, curruca de los jardines J^1; canaria IJo; piñata, /butrecilla/(buitrecilla) Ll; pinzoleta E.
430. Sylvia borin (Garden-warbler): curruca mosquitera BJ^2; curruca J?V; andahuertas J^1; picafigos LlJ^2.
431. Sylvia atricapilla (Blackcap): curruca capirotada BJ^2; curruca de cabeza negra EJ; pulverilla Jo; carbonero S; chimbo de maíz, pinzoleta E; picafigo, becafigo, papafigo, papahigo ?V.
432. Sylvia communis (Whitethroat): curruca zarcera BJ^2; curruca gris J^1; pastorcilla J.
433. Sylvia curruca (Lesser whitethroat): curruca zarcerilla BJ^2; curruca gris, curruca E; parlanchín J^1.
434. Sylvia nana (Desert-warbler): curruca sahariana B^2J^2.
435. Sylvia rüppelli (Rüppell's warbler): curruca de Rüppell B^2J^2.
436. Sylvia melanocephala (Sardinian warbler): curruca cabecinegra BJ^2; piroftalmo de cabeza negra J^1; carbonero S; palmera IJo; camara Jo.
437. Sylvia cantillans (Subalpine warbler): curruca carrasqueña BJ^2; curruca subalpina E; busqueta J^1.

438. Sylvia conspicillata (Spectacled warbler): curruca tomillera BJ^2;
curruca de anteojo J^1; curruca de anteojos J^2; friolenco J^1.

439. Sylvia undata (Dartford warbler): curruca rabilarga BJ^2;
pinzoletica J^1; jarero J^2; colorín, caganchina IJo.

440. Sylvia sarda (Marmora's warbler): curruca sarda JB.

441. Phylloscopus trochilus (Willow-warbler): mosquitero musical BJ^2;
mosquitero EJ; mosquitero común, mosquitera E; mosquilla IJo;
pinzoletica, /pinzoletita/E.

442. Phylloscopus collybita (Chiffchaff): mosquitero común BJ^2;
mosquitero Ll; mosquitero pardo E; mosquilla IJoJ; almendrita
JLl; pinzoletica EJ^2; chata E.

443. Phylloscopus bonelli (Bonelli's warbler): mosquitero papialbo BJ^2;
mosquitero de Bonelli J; mosquitero moruno E; mosquitero Ll.

444. Phylloscopus sibilatrix (Wood-warbler): mosquitero silbador BJ^2;
mosquitero verde E; /mosqueta/, zarcero EJ^1.

445. Phylloscopus fuscatus (Dusky warbler): mosquitero sombrío B^2J^2.

446. Phylloscopus schwarzi (Radde's willow-warbler): mosquitero de
Schwarz B^2J^2.

447. Phylloscopus inornatus (Yellow-browed warbler): mosquitero
bilistado B^2J^2; pinzoletica E.

448. Phylloscopus proregulus (Pallas's warbler): msoquitero de
Pallas B^2J^2.

449. Phylloscopus borealis (Arctic warbler): mosquitero boreal EB^2J^2.

450. Phylloscopus trochiloides (Greenish warbler): mosquitero
troquiloide B^2J^2.

451. Regulus regulus (Goldcrest): reyezuelo sencillo BJ^2; reyezuelo
EJ?A?PVD; régulo EV; estrelliña E; abadejo ?A?PV;
abadejo de invierno D; avica, castañeta ?A.
  451a. R. r. regulus (Goldcrest): reyezuelo sencillo genuino B^1.

452. Regulus ignicapillus (Firecrest): reyezuelo listado BJ^2; reyezuelo
JLl; /reyet/J^1; estrellina Jo; estrelliña E; castañita Ll;
abadejo de triple franja ?D.
  452a. R. i. teneriffae (—): reyezuelo sencillo tinerfeño B^1.

453. Cisticola juncidis (Fan-tailed warbler): buitrón $IJoLlBJ^2$;
/biutrecillo/(buitrecillo) I; cierrapuño IJoLl; cierra puño J^2;
tintín SIJo; tintín bolsicón E; bolsicón SC^3; chispita S; trepatorres,
tumanavilla I; cagachín J; cistícola común J^1.

Muscicapinae

454. Ficedula hypoleuca (Pied flycatcher): papamoscas cerrojillo BJ^2; cerrojillo IJoJLl; papamoscas luctuosa J^1; moscareta, chimbo de higuera E.

455. Ficedula albicollis (Collared flycatcher): papamoscas collarino BJ^2; papamoscas de collar E; moscareta de collar J; papamoscas V.

456. Ficedula narcissina (Narcissus flycatcher): papamoscas narciso B^2J^2.

457. Ficedula parva (Red-breasted flycatcher): papamoscas papirrojo BJ^2.

458. Muscicapa striata (Spotted flycatcher): papamoscas gris BJ^2; papamoscas $SIJoEJ^1Ll$; moscareta EJV; mosquitero LlJ^2; muscaria EV; muscicapa E; muscícapa V; piñata $SILlJ^2$.

459. Muscicapa latirostris (Brown flycatcher): papamoscas pardo B^2J^2.

Turdinae

460. Saxicola rubetra (Whinchat): tarabilla norteña BJ^2; tarabilla común J^1; cagarropa IJo; cagarropas S; cagaestacas E; caganchina IJo; zarzalera LlJ^2; sietearreldes J; picharchar E.

461. Saxicola dacotiae (Canary Islands stonechat): tarabilla canaria B^I.

462. Saxicola torquata (Stonechat): tarabilla común BJ^2; tarabilla de collar J; cagaestacas $ELlJ^2$; zarzalera IJo; chasco $TLlJ^2$; collalba EJ.

463. Oenanthe oenanthe (Wheatear): collalba gris BJ^2; collalba $ELlJ^2$; culiblanco IJoEJLl; coliblanco común E; ruiblanca $IJoELlJ^2$; rabiblanca J; peñasca LlJ^2; piornero E.

464. Oenanthe pleschanka (Pied wheatear): collalba pía B^2J^2.

465. Oenanthe hispanica (Black-eared wheatear): collalba rubia BJ^2; ruiblanca SIJo; coliblanco, culiblanco E; sacristán EJ; piñata LlJ^2.

466. Oenanthe deserti (Desert-wheatear): collalba desértica BJ^2.

467. Oenanthe isabellina (Isabelline wheatear): collalba Isabel B^2; collalba isabel J^2.

468. Oenanthe leucura (Black wheatear): collalba negra BJ^2; sacristán $IJoLlJ^2$; ruiblanca SI; culiblanco SJo; pedrero $IVeJoJ^2$; /pedreo/(pedrero) Ll; pájaro negro J.

469. Oenanthe leucopyga (White-rumped wheatear): collalba negra de Brehm B^2J^2.

73

470. Cercotrichas galactotes (Rufous warbler): alzacola SIJoELlBJ²; alzarrabo SJoE; rubita IJoLlJ²; pájaro rojo J; colirrojo SJo; colirrubio S; viñadera IJo.

471. Monticola saxatilis (Rock-thrush): roquero rojo BJ²; tordo de las rocas, solitario de las rocas J; /pasera de las rojes/E; mirlo pintado Jo; espantadizo LlJ².

472. Monticola solitarius (Blue rock-thrush): roquero solitario BJ²; solitario SIC⁴VeJoLlAJ²; solitario azul J; pájaro solitario EAV; pájaro loco EAV; tordo loco A.

473. Phoenicurus ochruros (Black redstart): colirrojo tizón BJ²; colirrojo negro J²; colirrojo SJoLlJ²; culirrojo I; cola roja J; tintorero IJo; carbonero IJoLlJ².

474. Phoenicurus phoenicurus (Redstart): colirrojo real BJ²; colirrojo EJLlAD; culirrojo IJo; culo rubio J¹; rabirrojo, chimbo de cola roja ED; solitaria D.

475. Phoenicurus moussieri (Moussier's redstart): colirrojo diademado B²J².

476. Erithacus rubecula (Robin): petirrojo IJoEJLlVDB; pitirrojo E; pechirrojo LlD; pechirrubio S; pechicolorado E; papirrojo E; paporrubio J²; papicolorado E; barbarroja J²; barba roja J¹; gargantirrojo S; pechel LlJ²; patiseco, pisco ELl; chamarreto LlJ²; sobrestante J; chindor, colorín, parpar, raitán E.

477. Luscinia megarhynchos (Nightingale): ruiseñor común BJ²; ruiseñor LlJoEJLlAPVD; silvarronco LlJ².

478. Luscinia luscinia (Thrush-nightingale): ruiseñor ruso B²J²; ruiseñor grande J¹; ruiseñor mayor D.

479. Luscinia calliope (Ruby-throat): ruiseñor calíope B²J².

480. Luscinia svecica (Bluethroat): pechiazul LlBJ²; gargantiazul SIJoJ; camancho Jo; /soldiya/(soldía, soldilla?) IJo; /flaveta/E.
    480a. L. s. cyanecula (White-spotted bluethroat): pechiazul medalla blanca B.
    480b. L. s. svecica (Red-spotted bluethroat): pechiazul medalla roja B.

481. Tarsiger cyanurus (Red-flanked bluetail): coliazul cejiblanco B²J².

482. Catharus minimus (Grey-cheeked thrush): zorzal carigrís B²J².

483. Catharus ustulatus (Olive-backed thrush): zorzal ustulado B²J².

484. Catharus guttatus (Hermit-thrush): zorzal colirrojo B²J².

485. Turdus unicolor (Tickell's thrush): zorzal unicolor B²J².

486. Turdus obscurus (Eye-browed thrush): zorzal rojigrís B²J².

487. Turdus ruficollis (see subspecies).
    487a. T. r. atrogularis (Black-throated thrush): zorzal papinegro B^2J^2.
    487b. T. r. ruficollis (Red-throated thrush): zorzal papirrojo B^2
488. Turdus naumanni (see subspecies).
    488a. T. n. eunomus (Dusky thrush): zorzal eunomo B^2J^2.
    488b. T. n. naumanni (Naumann's thrush): zorzal de Naumann B^2J^2.
489. Turdus pilaris (Fieldfare): zorzal real BJ^2; zorzal E; tordo castellano Sn; /tordella/E.
490. Turdus torquatus (Ring-ouzel): mirlo collarizo BJ^2; chirlo SIJoJ; capiblanco J.
    490a. T. t. torquatus (Ring-ouzel): mirlo collarizo nórdico B^1.
    490b. T. t. alpestris (Alpine ring-ouzel): mirlo collarizo serrano B^1.
491. Turdus merula (Blackbird): mirlo común EBJ^2; mirlo SIJoJLlVD; chirlomirlo P; mierla, mielra LlJ^2; merla, mirla EVD.
492. Turdus sibiricus (Siberian thrush): zorzal siberiano B^2J^2.
493. Turdus iliacus (Redwing): zorzal malvís B^2J^2; zorzal malvis B^1; zorzal C^2; malvis SIJo; malvís EAV; malviz EJ^1V; malvís alirrojo J^2; tordo alirrojo EAPV; /arandillo/, /trepajuncos/E.
494. Turdus philomelos (Song-thrush): zorzal común BJ^2; zorzal SC^2IJoEJLlA?PD; malvís cantábrico J^2; tordo $TEVJ^2$; tordo pardo J^2; tordo común ED; tordo músico E.
495. Turdus viscivorus (Mistle-thrush): zorzal charlo BJ^2; charla SIC^3JoEJLlAPV; charra, caga-aceite E; cagaaceite EAV; cagarrache V; tordo real J; tordo A; tordo mayor EAP; abiloria, bilorio LlJ^2; drena J; zorzal V.
496. Turdus migratorius (American robin): robín americano B^2J^2.
497. Zoothera dauma (Golden mountain-thrush): zorzal dorado BJ^2.

Timaliinae

498. Panurus biarmicus (Bearded tit): bigotudo JLlB.

PARULIDAE

499. Parula americana (Parula warbler): parula americana B^2J^2.
500. Dendroica virens (Black-throated green warbler): dendroica papinegra carigualda B^2J^2.
501. Mniotilta varia (Black-and-white warbler): niotilta varia B^2J^2.

VIREONIDAE

502. Vireo olivaceus (Red-eyed vireo): vireo ojirrojo B^2J^2; vireo aceitunado E.

AEGITHALIDAE

503. Aegithalos caudatus (Long-tailed tit): mito IJoJB; paro rabilargo J^1; rabilargo J^2; moscón de cola larga E; castañita LlJ^2; chamarón EVJ^2; acrédula ?E.

PARIDAE

Parinae

504. Parus palustris (Marsh-tit): carbonero palustre BJ^2; herrerillo SJ^1.
505. Parus montanus (Willow-tit): carbonero sibilino B^2J^2.
506. Parus lugubris (Sombre tit): carbonero lúgubre B^2J^2.
507. Parus cinctus (Siberian tit): carbonero lapón B^2J^2.
508. Parus cristatus (Crested tit): herrerillo capuchino BJ^2; capuchino IC^3JoJ; herrerillo moñudo J; paro moñudo J^1.
509. Parus ater (Coal-tit): carbonero garrapinos BJ^2; garrapinos Jo; garrapino, carbonero pequeño, carbonerillo J; herrerillo SJo; herreruelo, cerrojillo, cerrojito V; azabache ?AV; /primavera petita/E.
510. Parus caeruleus (Blue tit): herrerillo común BJ^2; herrerillo IJo?AV; paro azul, chamariz J; cerrajerillo, curita Ll; trepatroncos V; alionín ?E?APD; /primavera/ED.
    510a. P. c. caeruleus (Blue tit): herrerillo común europeo B^1.
    510b. P. c. teneriffae (—): herrerillo común africano B^1.
511. Parus cyanus (Azure tit): herrerillo cíaneo B^2J^2.
512. Parus major (Great tit): carbonero común BJ^2; carbonero $SIJoEJ^1$?A; paro carbonero ?AVD; carbonerito J; carbonerica A; carbonero mayor J^2; paro mayor J^1D; cerrajero IJo; cerrajillo SE; cerrojillo E; herrerillo $ELlDJ^2$; herreroche LlJ^2; carpintero IJo; guerrero I; quivevive IJo; fringilago V; catabejas, garrapinos, menseja E; capilla negra A.

Sittinae

513. Sitta europaea (Nuthatch): trepador azul BJ^2; trepatroncos
C^{3}JoEJ^{1}Ll; trepatroncos de Europa, sita europea E.
514. Sitta whiteheadi (Corsican nuthatch): trepador corso B^{2}J^2.
515. Sitta neumayer (Rock-nuthatch): trepador rupestre B^{2}J^2.

Tichodromadinae

516. Tichodroma muraria (Wall-creeper): treparriscos BJ^2;
pelarrocas J; arañero C^{3}EJLl; pájaro arañero EAPV.

CERTHIIDAE

517. Certhia familiaris (Tree-creeper): agateador norteño BJ^2;
agateador J^2; gateador J; trepatroncos SIC^{3}EJ; trepador EJ;
trepador familiar E; arañero SIC^{3}E; barba-jelena I.
518. Certhia brachydactyla (Short-toed tree-creeper): agateador común
BJ^2; agateador LlJ^2; gateador J^2; trepatroncos JoEJ; trepador EJ;
arañero Jo.

REMIZIDAE

519. Remiz pendulinus (Penduline tit): pájaro moscón IJoEJ?AVB;
moscón E.

PLOCEIDAE

520. Passer domesticus (House-sparrow): gorrión común EBJ^2; gorrión
doméstico ED; gorrión SITJoLl?AV; gurriato LlJ^2; pardal
ELlVDJ^2.
520a. P. d. italiae (Italian sparrow): gorrión italiano B^{2}J^2.
521. Passer hispaniolensis (Spanish sparrow): gorrión moruno SJoEBJ^2;
gorrión molinero EJ; molinero Jo.

77

522. Passer montanus (Tree-sparrow): gorrión molinero LlBJ²;
gorrión serrano IJoEJ.
523. Petronia petronia (Rock-sparrow): gorrión chillón BJ²; chilla JLl;
gorrión montés SIJo; gorrión campesino J.
524. Montifringilla nivalis (Snow-finch): gorrión alpino BJ².

FRINGILLIDAE

Fringillinae

525. Fringilla coelebs (Chaffinch): pinzón vulgar BJ²; pinzón
SIC³JoEJLlAVD; pinchón V; pinche, tintín LlJ²; pimpín T;
/pimpím/J²; peñato LlJ²; catachín, /triguera/A.
525a. F. c. coelebs (Continental chaffinch): pinzón común B¹.
525b. F. c. tintillon (Canarian chaffinch): pinzón vulgar
tintillón B¹.
526. Fringilla teydea (Canary Islands chaffinch): pinzón del Teide B¹.
527. Fringilla montifringilla (Brambling): pinzón real LlVBJ²;
pinzón EJ¹; montañés SIJo; millero IJo; /piñonero/V.

Carduelinae

528. Serinus citrinella (Citril finch): verderón serrano BJ²;
verdoncillo SJo; gafarrón ?EJ.
529. Serinus serinus (Serin): serín verdecillo B¹; serín J¹B²; cerín J¹;
verdecillo EJLl; chamaris (chamariz?) IJo; chamariz SE;
jilguerillo basto LlJ².
530. Serinus canaria (Canary): serín canario B¹; serín J²;
canario EAPV; canario silvestre, (f) canaria E.
531. Carduelis chloris (Greenfinch): verderón común BJ²;
verderón SEJLlAV; verdón SIC³JoEV; verderol, verdezuelo EV;
verdecillo APV; ruiseñor Ll; cardenal, chirriscla E.
532. Carduelis spinus (Siskin): lúgano IJB; lugano C³JoEAPV; lúbano
SJ²; lubano E; burano Ll; /chamariz/VD; /verderón/E.
533. Carduelis carduelis (Goldfinch): jilguero SIJoEJLlAVDB; (f)
jilguera E; silguero IEVD; sirguero EV; colorín, sietecolores
ELlAVJ²; pintadillo EVD; pintacilgo VD; soldadito LlJ²;
cardelina EVD; carbonero S.

78

534. Acanthis flavirostris (Twite): pardillo piquigualdo BJ²; pajarel J¹
535. Acanthis cannabina (Linnet): pardillo común BJ²; pardillo EJLlAPV; pardilla E; pardal EV; camacho SIC³Jo; /camachuelo/A; jamas IJo; pajarel EAV; gafarrón EA; pechicolorado V; pechirrojo EV; liñacero T.
536. Acanthis flammea (Redpoll): pardillo sizerín BJ²; pájaro linero J¹.
537. Acanthis hornemanni (Arctic redpoll): pardillo de Hornemann B²J².
538. Rhodopechys githaginea (Trumpeter-finch, Trumpeter bull-finch): camachuelo trompetero BJ².
539. Carpodacus erythrinus (Scarlet grosbeak): camachuelo carminoso BJ²; carpódaco carminoso J².
540. Carpodacus roseus (Rose-finch, Pallas's rose-finch): camachuelo róseo B²J².
541. Pinicola enucleator (Pine-grosbeak): camachuelo picogrueso B²J²; piquituerto de los abetos J¹; pico duro E.
542. Loxia pityopsittacus (Parrot crossbill): piquituerto lorito B²J²; cascapiñones J¹.
543. Loxia curvirostra (Crossbill): piquituerto común BJ²; piquituerto EJ¹?AV; pico-tuerto SIC³C⁴Jo; pico cruzado IJoEJ.
544. Loxia leucoptera (Two-barred crossbill): piquituerto franjeado B²; piquituerto de fajas blancas J¹.
545. Pyrrhula pyrrhula (Bullfinch): camachuelo común BJ²; camachuelo J¹V; pinzón real EJ?AD; piñonero ?A; frailecillo J; /esgrumador/J².
546. Coccothraustes coccothraustes (Hawfinch): picogordo BJ²; pico gordo IJoEJ¹Ll; piñonero SIJoEJ; pinzón real E; cascanueces SIJo.

EMBERIZIDAE

547. Emberiza calandra (Corn-bunting): triguero SC¹IJoEJLlB; triguero común J¹; gorrión triguero E; ave tonta IJoE?V; pájaro tonto EV; ave zonza ?V; escribiera Ll.
548. Emberiza citrinella (Yellowhammer): escribano cerillo BJ²; cerillo JoJ; ave tonta S; cip-cip, cité Ll; cite E; verderón de seto J¹; /verderón/, /verderol/D; citrinela E.
549. Emberiza leucocephala (Pine-bunting): escribano de Gmelin B²J².
550. Emberiza cia (Rock-bunting): escribano montesino BJ²; escribano IJoLlJ²; verderón loco J¹; cip J².

79

551. Emberiza cioides (Siberian meadow-bunting): escribano de Brandt B^2J^2.

552. Emberiza hortulana (Ortolan bunting, Ortolan): escribano hortelano BJ^2; hortelano EJLlAVD; hortolano IJoE; ave tonta S; cerillo Ll; /verdaula/E.

553. Emberiza cineracea (Grey-headed bunting, Cinereous bunting): escribano cinereo B^2; escribano cinéreo J^2.

554. Emberiza caesia (Cretzschmar's bunting): escribano ceniciento B^2J^2.

555. Emberiza cirlus (Cirl bunting): escribano soteño BJ^2; escribano JoLlJ^2; escribiera Ll; escribiente TJ^2; linacero IJoJ; ave tonta S; chilla Jo; cip-cip Ll; verderón /zizí/(cicí) J; verderón de vallado J^1.

556. Emberiza striolata (Striped bunting): escribano sahariano B^1.

557. Emberiza pusilla (Little bunting): escribano pigmeo BJ^2.

558. Emberiza chrysophrys (Yellow-browed bunting): escribano cejigualdo B^2J^2.

559. Emberiza rustica (Rustic bunting): escribano rústico B^2J^2.

560. Emberiza aureola (Yellow-breasted bunting): escribano aureolado B^2J^2; ave tonta J^1.

561. Emberiza rutila (Chestnut bunting): escribano herrumbroso B^2J^2.

562. Emberiza melanocephala (Black-headed bunting): escribano cabecinegro B^2J^2.

563. Emberiza bruniceps (Red-headed bunting): escribano carirrojo B^2J^2.

564. Emberiza spodocephala (Black-faced bunting): escribano enmascarado B^2J^2.

565. Emberiza schoeniclus (Reed-bunting): escribano palustre BJ^2; molinero, hortolano Jo; matinero J^2.

566. Junco hyemalis (Slate-coloured junco): junco pizarroso B^2J^2.

567. Passerella iliaca (Fox-sparrow): chingolo zorruno B^2J^2.

568. Zonotrichia albicollis (White-throated sparrow): chingolo gorgiblanco B^2J^2.

569. Calcarius lapponicus (Lapland bunting): escribano lapón B^2J^2.

570. Plectrophenax nivalis (Snow-bunting): escribano nival BJ^2; plectrófano de las nieves J^1.

Glossary: Part II

abadejo   (1) nonsp 451 [and 452] goldcrests; (2) [nonsp 380+ wagtails]
— de invierno   451
— — triple franja   bkn 452 (?)
abanto   (1) pop sp 107; (2) improp? reg? conf? 109
abejaruco   (1) pop sp 334; (2) off pop nonsp/gen/fam 334-335 bee-
    eaters; (3) [Mex nonsp? tyrants gen *Tyrannus*]
— bigotudo   bkn 335
— común   off 334
— papirrojo   off 335
abejero   reg var abejaruco 334 [note reg vars Sal abajarruco, Leon
    abejarruco, Murcia abejeruco, abejoruco, etc.]
abiloria   495
[abión   Co Ast = avión 325? 352?]
abubilla   (1) off pop 337; (2) off pop nonsp/gen/fam hoopoes
— común   bkn 337
[abubillo   reg var abubilla]
abuja, abujeta   pop 205
aburraca   var urraca 393
abutarda   var avutarda 177
[abutardo   Sal buitre 108?]
[acacalote   Mex = somorgujo 5-8?]
accípiter, accípitre, accipíter, accipitre   (1) arch nonsp hawks, falcons;
    (2) bkn scl 122; (3) bkn gen 122-124
acéntor   var acentor
acentor   off scl gen/fam 404-406 accentors
— alpino   off 404
— común   off 406
— de bosque   bkn 406
— — los Alpes   bkn scl 404
— — mejillas negras   bkn 405
— — Pallas   off 405
— silvestre   bkn 406
acrédula   (1) 503?; (2) [Sal = cogujada 364?, 365?]
agachadera   var Andal+ agachadiza 196, 198

agachadiza   (1) off pop nonsp/gen^2 196-198 snipe;   (2) pop sp esp 196 and 198
— chica   off 198
— común   off 196
— doble, a. grande, a. mayor   bkn 197
— menor, a. pequeña   bkn 198
— real   off pop 197
— sorda   198
agachona   reg var Andal Am agachadiza 196+
agarrapatosa   pop var garrapatosa 44
agateador   (1) off gen 517-518 tree-creepers;   (2) pop sp esp 518; (3) pop reg conf? 343 +?
— común   off 518
— norteño   off 517
aguanieve   f var aguanieves 380a
aguanieves   f (1) 380a;   (2) 183
águila   (1) pop nonsp 111+ eagles, buzzards, sea-eagles, harriers, etc; (2) off gen^4 111-118, 135-136;   (3) pop sp Andal 110
— acciptrina   bkn 117
— barbuda   110
— bastarda   bkn? 118
— blanca   (1) pop Cast +? nonsp? conf? 107, 117, 118;   (2) bkn? conf? 136
— blancuzca   pop Andal 117
— calzada   off pop 118
— caudal, a. caudalosa   bkn? 111
— chillona   bkn 116
— — mayor   bkn 114
— chivata   110
— chivera   111
— común   bkn 111
— conejera   bkn? 118
— culebrera   off pop 135
— de Bonelli   bkn 117
— — cabeza blanca   bkn 129
— — estepa, a. de las estepas   bkn 115
— — las rocas   pop Andal 111 and conf? 117
— — los árboles   pop Andal 112
— — moros   pop Andal 130
— — ribera   131

águila de río   bkn? 136
— dorada   bkn 111
— enana   bkn? 118
— gallinera   bkn? 124
— imperial   off 112
— leona   pop Andal +? 128
— liebrera   bkn? 117
— maculada   bkn 114
— manchada   bkn 116
— marina   [Cat] 128
— — grande   128
— melión   pop Andal 135; v. also melión
— moteada   off 114
— negra   (1) pop 111; (2) pop reg conf? 112
— nipalense   bkn scl 115
— parda   pop 135
— perdicera   off pop 117
— perdiguera   var a. perdicera 117
— pescadora   (1) off pop 136; (2) improp 128
— pintada   pop 117
— pomerana   off scl 116
— rapaz   off scl 113
— ratera, a. ratonera   bkn? 119
— real   (1) off pop 111; (2) pop reg conf? 112; cf. águila negra
— serpentaria   135
aguililla   (1) pop nonsp for smaller "águilas" (e.g. buzzards, Osprey);
    (2) [reg = cernícalo 146 (?)]
— pescadora   136
— ratonera   119
aguiloria   /?/ 107
aguilucho   (1) pop sp 131 +?; (2) off gen 131-134 harriers; (3) pop
    conf? 118; (4) young of águila: eaglet +
— cenizo   off 134
— lagunero   off 131
— pálido   off 132
— papialbo   off 133
[aguión   Co Ast = avión 325? 352?]
aguja   off pop nonsp/gen 205-206 godwits
— colinegra   off 205
— colipinta   off 206

agujeta   (1) pop nonsp 205 [and 206] godwits; (2) pop sp 205; v. also
    abujeta
— gris   off 220
aguzanieve   f var aguzanieves 380a
aguzanieves   f 380a
airón   39
[alabanco, alavanco   var lavanco 91?]
[alandrina   Co Ast = alondra 367?]
albatros   (1) nonsp/fam 10-14 albatrosses; (2) improp sp 10
— cabecigrís   off 13
— común   bkn 10
— clororrinco   off scl 12
— de párpados negros   bkn 11
— — pico amarillo   bkn 12
— ojeroso   off 11
— sombrío   off 14
— viajero   off 10
alca   (1) off scl 282; (2) bkn scl fam 282-284 auks
— común   off 282
— enana   bkn 284
— gigante   bkn 283
alcaraván   (1) off pop 241; (2) Guipúzcoa 201; (3) conf /48/ [and
    others]
— común   bkn 241
alcatraz   m (1) pop 32; (2) pop Am nonsp/fam/gen 37-38 pelicans;
    (3) [pop Am sp Brown pelican, *Pelecanus occidentalis*]; (4) pop reg
    larger gulls
— común   off 32
alcaudón   (1) off pop nonsp/gen 381-385 shrikes; (2) pop sp esp 383
— chico   off 384
— común   off 383
— dorsirrojo   off 381
— isabel, a. Isabel   off scl 381a
— menor   bkn 383
— núbico   off 382
— picanzo   improp? sp 385 [cf. Port picanço nonsp 381-385 shrikes]
— real   off pop 385
— — meridional   off scl 385b
— — moruno   off 385c
— — nórdico   off 385a

alcedón   bkn 333
[álcido   bkn scl 282-290 auks]
alción   bkn poet 333
alcotán   off pop 137
— palomero   bkn? 143
[aldorta   ?]
aleto   136; v. also halieto
alfaneque   conf (1) arch and Port +? 139; (2) /146/; (3) /119/
alfaneto   var alfaneque /146/ [139?]
alfarfera   pop Murcia 374 [and 376? cf. alfarfero]
alfarfero   376 [and 374? cf. alfarfera]
[alferraz   falcon   ?]
[alforre   falcon   ?]
[alforrocho   Arag = gavilán 122?]
alhoja   [Val alóixa] 367
alimocha   reg var Cast Andal +? alimoche 107
alimoche   pop 107
— común   off 107
alionín   510
almendrita   pop nonsp? conf? various small birds 403, 442, [+]
— de verano   pop 424
[aloda   Arag = alondra, calandria 367? 359? +?]
alondra   (1) pop sp 367; (2) pop sp conf? 359; (3) off gen^4 in
   compounds 355, 356, 362-363 larks (−); (4) bkn pop nonsp in
   compounds as (3) plus 364, 366 larks; 371, 374 pipits; and 404
   accentor
— común   off 367
— cornuda   off 362
— — lapona   off 362a
— — sahariana   off 363
— de campo   367
— — Dupont   off scl 356
— — las rocas   404
— — los bosques   bkn scl 366
— — — campos   bkn scl 367
— — — prados   bkn 374
— — monte   pop 366
— ibis   off 355
— moñuda   bkn? 364
— pipí   bkn? 371

[alondrilla   reg = curruca 430? 433?]
/alosa/   Cat 367
/alova/   Cat 367 [Cat 364, 365]
[aloya   Burgos Logroño = alondra 367?]
alucón   bkn scl 314
alzacola   off pop 470
[alzacolas   Murcia = aguzanieves 380?]
alzarrabo   pop 470
ampélido   bkn scl (1) fam waxwings; (2) sp 401
ampelis   bkn scl 401
— europeo   off 401
ánade   (1) bkn gen+ ducks (−); (2) off gen− 55, 62-65; (3) sp
    esp 55
— común   bkn 55
— cristado de ribera   bkn 70
— friso   off 62
— rabudo   off 65
— real   off 55
— salvaje /collvert/   55
— silbón   off 63
— — americano   off 64
— vulgar   bkn 55
andahuertas   430
andarina   reg Ast + 350
andarrío   Arag var andarríos 187
andarríos   (1) off pop nonsp 207-211, 219 sandpipers; (2) pop nonsp
    185, 187 [+] plovers (−); (3) pop reg sundry river-birds 333,
    380a, 402
— bastardo   off 208
— chico   off 210
— de Kent   bkn 187
— /de/ (del) Terek   off 219
— grande   off 207
— maculado   off 211
— pequeño   bkn 186
— solitario   off scl 209
andolina   Sal 350
andorina   W 350
[andoriña   Gal 350, cf. Port andorinha]
[andrulina   Co Ast = /?/alondra 367?]

anduriña W 350
[andurlina reg 350] v. also andarina, arandela
ánima pop Andal + ? 20
ánsar (1) off gen 92-97 geese (−), grey geese (+); (2) improp? sp
   92, 95
— blanco Mex 97
— braquirrinco bkn scl 96
— campestre off scl 95
— careto chico off 94
— — grande off 93
— cenizo bkn 92
— común off 92
— — occidental off 92a
— — oriental off 92b
— frentialbo chico bkn 94
— — grande bkn 93
— hiperbóreo bkn scl 97
— nival off 97
— piquicorto off scl 96
— real Mex 97
anserata pop? Andal? 90
apuranieves 380a
arán mispr? arau/arao 285
[arandela Álava 350]
arandillo (1) 416?; (2) /493/; v. also trepajuncos
arañero (1) pop 516; (2) pop nonsp? or conf? 517-518; v. also pájaro
   arañero
arao off pop? gen 285-287 guillemots
— aliblanco off 287
— común off 285
— de Brünnich off 286
/arau/ var arao 285 [cf. Port arau, airó, aire nonsp guillemots]
arcea 199
archibebe (1) off pop Andal+ nonsp/gen− 212-218 —shanks, —legs,
   sandpipers (−); (2) pop sp esp 212
— claro off 216
— común off 212
— fino off 217
— oscuro off 213
— paticorto off scl 218

archibebe patigualdo chico   off scl Eng 215
— — grande   off Eng 214
arciucha   196
árdea   (1) [bkn scl gen 39+ herons]; (2) /241/
ardea menor   (1) bkn 46; (2) [= garza 39?, alcaraván 241?]
arenatela   /?/ 222
arenosa   207
aro   mispr? arao 285
arpella   (1) pop [and Cat] 131; (2) pop Andal +? conf? 119
[arrapapájaros   Nav = milano 125?]
[arrecájel(e)], arrejaco, arrejaque, [arrejáquele]   (1) 325; (2) [Sal+ =
   vencejo, avión 352?]
arrendajo   (1) pop 391; (2) off gen^2 390, 391 jays
— común   off 391
— funesto   off 390
— glandívoro   bkn scl 391
[arricángel   Sal = vencejo 325? 352?]
ascle   /?/ 62
atahorma   135
/aureneta/   Cat 350
autillo   conf (1) off 308; (2) error? 314; (3) /317/
avanto   var abanto 107
[avecasina   (1) Am var becacina 196-198; (2) /Am = becada 199/]
avecilla de las nieves   380a
ave de cuchar, a. de cuchara   bkn? 52
— — las tempestades   pop 18
— — San Martín   pop 132
— — — Pedro   pop 18
— fría   var avefría 183
avefría   off pop 183
— espolada   off 184
— vistosa   191
avetarda   var avutarda 177
ave tonta   pop nonsp/gen/fam 547, 548, 552, 555, 560 + buntings
avetorillo   off gen 46-47 little bitterns, dwarf bitterns
— común   off 46
— de Sturm   off 47
ave toro, ave-toro   var avetoro 48
avetoro   (1) pop 48; (2) nonsp 46-49 bitterns; (3) off gen 48-49
   bitterns (−)

avetoro común   off 48
— lentiginoso   off scl 49
ave zonza   var ave tonta 547 + buntings
avica   Álava 451 [452?]
avión   (1) pop nonsp/gen 325-327 [+] swifts;   (2) off pop nonsp/
    fam— 348, 349, 352 martins;   (3) pop sp esp 352
— común   off 352
— de pecho blanco   pop? 327
— real   pop 327
— roquero   off scl 349
— rupestre   bkn scl 349
— zapador   off 348
avoceta   off pop 237
— común   bkn 237
avucasta, avucastro   arch 177
avutarda   off pop 177
— mayor   bkn 177
— menor   bkn Eng? 178
azabache   509
azor   (1) off pop 124;   (2) conf? /118/
— de las zuritas   124
azulejo   pop various blue birds (1) 333;   (2) 334;   (3) 336
azulillo   pop 333
azulón   pop? 55

baharí   (1) 138b;   (2) /138c/ v. halcón baharí
baquiñuela   237
barba-jelena   /?/ 517
barba roja, barbarroja   476
[barbón   pop 177]
barbudo   110
barnacla   off gen 100-103 black geese
— canadiense   off 102
— cariblanca   off 101
— carinegra   off 100
— cuellirroja   off 103
becacica   var mispr? becacina 196
becacina   (1) pop NE 196 +?;   (2) bkn pop? nonsp/gen² 196-198
  snipe

becacina grande   bkn 197
— mediana   bkn 196
— pequeña   bkn 198
becada, becada común   (1) bkn? [pop Cat] 199; (2) /196/
becafigo   (1) 431 (?) [430?] v. also papafigo; (2) [386?] cf. becafigos
becafigos   (1) pop reg 386; (2) [431?, 430?] cf. becafigo
[becardín   Arag=becada pequeña   ?]
[becardón   Arag=agachadiza 196? 198?]
[becaza   Co reg=chocha 199]
[bernacha   bkn gen 100-103 black geese cf. Port bernacho]
— de collar   bkn 100
[bernicla   bkn gen 100-103 black geese]
bigotudo   (1) off pop 498; (2) pop reg 137
bilorio   495
bisbita   m (1) pop nonsp? or not distinguished? 371, 374; (2) off gen
   368-376 pipits
— arbóreo   off 371
— caminero   off 370
— campestre   off 369
— común   off 374
— de Hodgson   off scl 372
— del Petchora   off 373
— de Richard   off 368
— gorgirrojo   off 375
— ribereño   off 376
— — alpino   off 376a
— — costero   off 376b
— — — nórdico   off 376c
bitor   170
/biutrecillo/   mispr buitrecillo 453
blanca   Murc 393
— de los arroyos   /?/ 380a
boceta   var mishearing? avoceta 237
/boix/   Cat? 71
bolsicón   pop reg 453
bonasa   mispr? bonasia bkn scl 153
[bonasia   bkn scl 153]
boñiguero   107
borní   (1) 139; (2) /131/ v. halcón borní
/bragat/   Cat? 66

branta rojiza   bkn improp? 68 (cf. *Branta* scl gen 100-103)

bruja   pop? 307

buarillo   308

buaro   (1) var buharro 308; (2) /?/145; (3) /137/

[bubarro   Nav = buharro 308?]

bubía   bkn gen 32+ gannets and boobies

[bubilla], bubillo   reg vars abubilla 337

bubulco   bkn scl 44

[bubulilla], bubupa   reg vars abubilla 337

buharro   308

buho   (1) pop sp 309; (2) pop sp 317; (3) off pop nonsp in compounds 308, 309, 310, 317 owls (−)

— chico   off 317

— común   bkn 317

— de orejas largas   bkn 317

— grande   pop reg 309

— mediano   bkn 317

— nival   off 310

— pequeño   (1) pop? 317; (2) bkn 308

— real   off pop 309

buitre   (1) pop sp 108; (2) improp 107; (3) bkn pop? nonsp/fam 107-110 vultures

buitrecilla   /?/429 [453?]

buitrecillo   pop Andal 453

buitre común   off bkn 108

— franciscano   (1) pop 108; (2) improp 109 (etym inappropriate) verbal conf? with buitre monje and scl

— leonado   bkn? 108

— monje   109

— negro   off pop 109

buitrón   off pop 453

bújaro   pop reg? 309

bujo   var Andal +? buho (1) 309; (2) 317

— real   var Andal +? buho real 309

burano   532

busardo   (1) 119; (2) bkn gen 131-134 harriers; v. also buzardo

buscarla   (1) pop Cat nonsp/gen [416, 417, 420], 421 reed-warblers; (2) off gen 409-414 grasshopper-warblers

— de Gray   off 409

— — Pallas   off 412

buscarla fluvial   off scl 411
— lanceolada   bkn scl 414
— pinta   bkn 413
— pintoja   off 413
— unicolor   off 410
buso   119
[busquereta   Andal 437?]
busqueta   437
butrecilla   var mispr? buitrecilla 429
buzardo   bkn gen 131?-134 harriers
— azulado   bkn 132
— ceniciento   bkn 134
— pálido   bkn 133
buzo   gen 119+ buzzards
— común   bkn 119
— patudo   bkn 120

caballero   bkn Fr (chevalier) gen 207+ sandpipers
— culo blanco   bkn 207
— de los estanques   bkn 217
— /gambetta/   error Italian 212
— gris   bkn 216
— pardo   bkn 213
— silvestre, c. silvícola   bkn 208
cabezón   (1) pop 71; (2) pop Andal +? 391
cabezota   383
/cabrellot blanc/, /cabrellot/blanco   Cat? 4
/cadellot/   Cat? 4
cagaaceite   pop 495
cagachín   453
cagaestacas   pop nonsp? or not distinguished? 460, 462
[caganchín   Andal var cagachín 453?]
caganchina   (1) pop Andal 439; (2) verbal conf? with cagarropas 460
cágalo   (1) pop nonsp/gen/fam 246-249 skuas; (2) pop conf? 270
cagarrache   495
cagarropa, cagarropas   pop 460
cajaílla   pop reg 358
cajonera   pop Andal +? 337
caladre   (1) 359; (2) error? 367
calamón   (1) pop sp 171; (2) off gen^2 171-173 gallinules

calamón común   off 171
— de Allen   off 173
— dorsiverde   off 172
/calandreta/   Cat 357
calandria   (1) pop sp 359;   (2) error? 365;   (3) off gen 359-361
   larks (−)
— aliblanca   off scl 360
— común   off 359
— de los campos   359
— — — montes   366
— negra   off 361
calandrina   mispr?   calandriña (cf. Port calandrinha) error? 369 (cf.
   Port 359)
calcidrán real   bkn? 384
calidris   bkn scl gen 222+ stints (+)
— de los arenales   bkn scl 233
camacho   pop reg 535
camachuelo   (1) pop sp 545;   (2) off gen⁴ 538, 539-540, 541, 545;
   (3) verbal conf? with camacho 535
— carminoso   off scl 539
— común   off 545
— picogrueso   off 541
— róseo   off 540
— trompetero   off 538
camancho   mispr? camacho 480
camara   /?/ 436
camaronero   (1) pop reg 333;   (2) [Am other kingfishers fam *Alcedini-
   dae*]
canaria   (1) f of canario 530;   (2) pop Andal conf? 429
canario   (1) pop 530;   (2) pop reg 334 (?);   v. also serín canario 530
canastela   Andal var canastera 243
canastera   (1) off pop sp 243;   (2) off gen 243-244 pratincoles
— alinegra   off 244
cangrejera   (1) pop 43;   (2) pop conf? 48;   (3) pop conf? 46
cangrejerita   pop Andal +? 46
canut   /?/ 221
cañamera   420
[cañamero   (1) Andal Nav = pardillo 535?;   (2) Álava = verderón 531?]
capacho   arch? (1) 45;   (2) 322 [and 321?] cf. zumaya
capiblanco   490

capilla negra   arch 512
capitán   pop Andal + ? 59
— caretón   (carretón? cf. cerceta carretona 59) pop Andal + ? 59
capuchino   pop Andal + ? 508
carabinera   Sal 364
cárabo   (1) off pop sp 314; (2) pop reg sp 317; (3) pop reg (conf?
    with 314) 318; (4) /307/; (5) /311/; (6) off gen 314-316
    owls (−)
— común   off 314
— lapón   off 315
— uralense   off scl 316
cara de juez   pop reg? 65
carambolo sereño   194; v. also chorlito carambolo 194
carbonerica   Álava 512
carbonerillo   [Andal + ?] 509
carbonerito   512
carbonero   (1) pop sp 512;   (2) off gen − in compounds 504-507, 509,
    512 tits (−); (3) pop reg sp other small black, black-capped birds
    431, 436, 473, 533
— común   off 512
— garrapinos   off 509
— lapón   off 507
— lúgubre   off scl 506
— mayor   bkn scl 512
— palustre   off scl 504
— pequeño   bkn 509
— sibilino   off scl 505
cardelina   533
cardenal   (1) /?/ 531; (2) [Am sp/gen Cardinal, *Richmondena cardi-
    nalis* and subsps]
/cargolet/   Cat 403
/carisalero/   mispr carrisalero, carrizalero 422, 424
[carlanca   336?]
carlanco   (1) pop Andal + ? 336; (2) [/ = zancuda/   ?]
carnero del Cabo   pop 10
carniza   pop reg 403
carolo   pop reg 282
carpintero   (1) pop reg 338; (2) pop Andal 512
carpódaco carminoso   bkn scl 539
carraca   off pop 336

/carrán/ mispr charrán 274

[carranca var carlanca 336?]

[carrancho / = mohino 392/ 336?]

carranco var carraca×carlanco?, mispr? carlanco 336

carrecera grande mispr? carricera 422; cf. carricerín, carricero, carrizalero

/carregadet/ Cat? 208

carregadora 243

carretera (1) pop nonsp? or not distinguished? 364, 365; (2) 58

carricerín off nonsp in compounds 415, 416, 417, warblers (−)

— cejudo off 416

— común off 417

— real off 415

carricero off gen− 418-422 reed-warblers

— agrícola off scl 418

— común off 421

— de Blyth off 419

— poliglota off scl 420

— tordal off 422

carrión /?/ 304

carrisalero var Andal? carrizalero (1) 422; /?/ 424

carrizalero (1) pop 422; (2) /?/ 424

carrizo (1) 403; (2) [Ast /?/ "parecido al jilguero" ?]

[cascahuesos Sant "ave de rapiña" ?]

cascanueces (1) off 394; (2) pop Andal +? 546

cascapiñones /542/, [541? 543?]

[castañero (1)/ = genus Colymbus (i.e. Gavia 1-4/; (2) var? canastera 243]

castañeta Álava 451? [452?]

castañita pop reg (1) 403; (2) 452; (3) 503

catabejas pop Álava 512

catachín Álava 525

catalinita pop reg 277

cataraña 41?

caudatrémula arch 380a

caudón arch and reg var alcaudón 383 +?

cencerillo pop reg 267

cenizo (1) pop Andal Nav +? 71; (2) pop Andal +? nonsp? or not distinguished? 132, 134

cerceta (1) pop sp esp 57; (2) pop reg 59; (3) off gen− 56-61 teals

cerceta aliazul   off 56
— carretona   off 59
— común   (1) off 57; (2) bkn 59
— de alas azules   bkn? Mex 56
— — alfanjes   off 61
— — invierno   57
— del Baikal   off 60
— de lista verde   bkn? Mex 57
— mayor   bkn 59
— menor   bkn 57
— pardilla   off 58
cerillo   (1) pop 548; (2) conf? 552
cerín   var mispr? serín 529
cernícalo   (1) pop 146; (2) improp? conf? 122; (3) off gen— falcons
   (−), kestrels (+)
— común   bkn 146
— patirrojo   off 144
— primilla   off 145
— vulgar   off 146
— yanqui   off 147
cerrajerillo   (1) /?/ 510 cf. cerrojillo 512; (2) [Álava = reyezuelo 451,
   452?]
cerrajero   (1) pop Andal 512; (2) [Álava = calandria 359?]; (3) [Sant
   = cerrojillo 512?, /herrerillo/ 510?]
cerrajillo   var cerrojillo 512
[cerrenícale   (1) Sal = /?/ gavilán 122?; (2) var cernícalo 146?]
[cerrica   Ast "ave diminuta" ?]
cerrojillo   pop (1) 454; (2) nonsp? or conf? 509, 512
cerrojito   509 [512?]
[cháchara   ?]
chamaris   orthog error chamarís, chamariz 529
[chamarís   var chamariz ?]
chamariz   m (1) pop 529; (2) /?/ 510; (3) /532/
[chamarizo   Andal var chamariz 529?]
chamarón   503
chamarreto   476
charadrio   (1) [bkn scl gen 185-194 plovers (−)]; (2) /241/
charla   pop 495
charra   (1) reg var charla 495; (2) [Nav = /?/ malviz 493];
   (3) [Andal = /?/ mirlo 491]; (4) /?/ 158; (5) [Nav = grajo ?]

charrán   (1) pop improp? sp 279; (2) off pop? gen² 272-280 terns (—);
    (3) pop Andal +? 187
— ártico   off 273
— bengalés   off scl 280
charrancito   off 277
charrán común   off 272
— de Dougall   bkn scl 274
— embridado   off 276
— gigante   off 278
— pardelo   off 281
— patinegro   off 279
— rosado   off 274
— sombrío   off 275
chasco   pop Gal +? improp? sp 462 [cf. Port nonsp? conf? 460,
    462, 463]
chata   442
chepecha   403
chilla   (1) pop? 523; cf. gorrión chillón; (2) 555
[chimbo   pop Vizcaya nonsp "bird"   ?]
— de cola roja   Vizcaya 474
— — higuera   Vizcaya 454
— — maíz   Vizcaya 431
— hormiguero   Vizcaya 347
— real   Vizcaya 383
chimita   pop Álava 380a
chindor   476
[chincol, chingol   pop Am var chingolo]
[chingolo   pop Am nonsp/gen *Zonotrichia, Passerella* +?]
— gorgiblanco   off 568
— zorruno   off 567
[chirivín   Extrem "pájaro pequeño" ?]
chirlerona   359
[chirlito   reg var chorlito 191+]
chirlo   pop Andal +? 490
chirlomirlo   (1) /?/ 491 [490?]; (2) [Sal = tordo ?]
chirriscla   /?/ 531
chirta   367
chispita   453
chocha   (1) pop 199; (2) /196/
chocha perdiz   off pop 199

chochaperdiz   var chocha perdiz 199
chochín   off pop 403
chochita   var chochín 403
chorcha   var chocha 199
[chorla   "especie de ganga" 291?]
chorlitejo   off gen— 185-190 ringed plovers
— asiático   off scl 189
— chico   off 186
— culirrojo   off 188
— grande   off 185
— mongol   off 190
— patinegro   off 187
chorlito   (1) pop nonsp/fam 181-194 plovers; (2) off nonsp in com-
    pounds 181-182, 191-194 plovers (—); (3) pop sp esp 191 and 192;
    (4) /?/ reg? 241; (5) conf /217/
— carambolo   off 194
— coliblanco   off 181
— de collar   bkn 185
— dorado   bkn 192
— — chico   off 193, 193a
— — común   off 192
— gris   off 191
— marismeño   pop? 194
— siberiano   off 193b
— social   off scl 182
chotacabras   (1) pop nonsp? or not distinguished? 321, 322 (if sp 322
    rather than 321); (2) off fam 321-324 nightjars
— de collar rojo   bkn 322
— egipcio   off 323
— gris   off 321
— pardo   off 322
— yanqui   off 324
chova   conf (1) pop nonsp? conf? 395, [396?], 397, 398, 399a, 399b
    crows (±); (2) off gen 395-396 choughs
— piquiamarilla   bkn 396
— piquigualda   off 396
— piquirroja   off 395
churlita   223
churra   (1) pop 291; (2) pop reg conf 366, 367; (3) error? 230
churrica   (1) 357 (?); (2) 368 (?)

churrilla . conf? (1) 233; (2) 222 [cf. 223]
— de tres dedos   233
— minuta   bkn 223
churruca   406
[cicí   555? cf. cip-cip]
[ciensayos   "de plumaje de colores diversos" ?]
cierra puño, cierrapuño   pop reg 453
cigoñuela   var cigüeñuela 238
cigüeña   (1) off pop nonsp/fam 50-51 storks; (2) pop sp 50
— blanca   bkn 50
— común   off 50
— negra   off pop 51
cigüenela   pop var cigüeñuela
cigüeñuela   off pop 238
cigüiñuela   var cigüeñuela
ciguiñuela   var mispr? cigüiñuela
[ciguñuela   arch var cigüeñuela]
cinceta   pop nonsp/gen 368, 369, 371, 374, 375 [+] pipits
cinguinela   var mispr? cigüeñuela 238
cip   (cip-cip?) /?/ 550 [548?, 555?]
cip-cip   pop conf? nonsp? (1) 548; (2) 555
circaeto   bkn scl 135
cisne   (1) off pop nonsp/gen 104-106 swans; (2) sp 104; (3) improp
   sp 105
— cantor   off 105
— chico   off 106
— chiflador   Mex 106
— común   104
— de Bewick   off 106
— doméstico ordinario   104 ("name" or description?)
— manso   bkn? 104
— mudo   bkn scl 104
— salvaje, c. silvestre   105
— vulgar   off 104
cistícola común   bkn scl 453
cite, cité   548
citrinela   bkn scl 548
clángula histriónico (histriónica?)   bkn scl 80
— vulgar   bkn scl 73
coalla   (1) 199; (2) [arch = codorniz 159]

cochevís   bkn? (cf. French cochevis) 364

codorniz   off pop 159

— canaria   off 159b

— común   off 159a

cogujada   (1) pop nonsp? or not distinguished? 364, 365; (2) off gen
364-365 larks (−)

— común   off 364

— montesina   off 365

cogullada   Cat +? var cogujada 364, 365

cola roja   473

coletero   403

coliazul cejiblanco   off 481

coliblanco   pop nonsp/gen 463, 465+ wheatears; v. also culiblanco

— común   bkn 463

colimbo   bkn scl gen/fam 1-4 divers

— ártico   off scl 1

— chico   off 4

— de Adams   off scl 3

— glacial   bkn 2

— grande   off 2

— menor   bkn 1

colirrojo   (1) off pop nonsp/gen 473-475 redstarts; (2) pop sp esp
473; (3) pop reg 470

— diademado   off 475

— negro   bkn 473

— real   off 474

— tizón   off 473

colirrubio   470

collalba   (1) pop improp? sp 463; (2) off pop? gen 463-469 wheatears; (3) conf? 462

— desértica   off scl 466

— gris   off 463

— Isabel   off scl 467

— negra   off 468

— — de Brehm   off 469

— pía   off 464

— rubia   off 465

colorín   conf? (1) pop reg 533; (2) pop Andal 439; (3) /?/476

combatiente   off pop 236

— común   bkn 236

copada   364

copetuda   conf 364 (?), 367 (?)

— totovía   (totovía copetuda?) 364

coquinero   pop Andal +? 79

[corconera   (1) Sant "cierto ánade" ? ; (2) Sant "cuervo marino" 33?
   34?]

cormorán   (1) off bkn fam/gen 33-35 cormorants; (2) sp 33

— común   bkn 33

— enano   bkn scl 35

— grande   off 33

— — chino   off scl 33b

— — nórdico   off 33a

— moñudo   off 34

— — atlántico   off 34a

— — sardo   off 34b

cormorano   var cormorán 33 +

cormorán pigmeo   off scl 35

corneja   (1) off pop 399; (2) pop 308, cf. corneta

— blanca   /397/ sense unacceptable [399b?]

— calva   398

— cenicienta   off 399b

— de campanario   bkn 397

— negra   off 399a

corneta   pop var corneja (2) 308

cornichuela   308

[correcamina   Sal = cogujada 364, 365]

correcaminos   364 [and 365?]

corredor   off 245

— de Europa, c. isabela   bkn 245

correlimos   off nonsp esp gen *Calidris* 221-232, and 233-235 stints (+),
   sandpipers (±)

— acuminado   off 228

— canelo   off 235

— común   off 230

— de Baird   off scl 227

— — Bartram   off 200

— — Bonaparte   off 226

— — Temminck   off scl 225

— falcinelo   off scl 234

— gordo   off 221

correlimos menudillo   off scl 224
— menudo   off scl 223
— oscuro   off 222
— pectoral   off 229
— semipalmeado   off 232
— tridáctilo   off scl 233
— zarapitín   off 231
correplaya   pop Andal + ? 185 + ?
correríos   pop Andal + ? 185 + ?
corteza   pop 291
coruja   var curuja nonsp? conf (1) 307; (2) 308; (3) [Port nonsp
   owls (−); sp 317]
corvejón   bkn? 33
[cotán   Co Sal var alcotán 137]
cotorra   393
/cotorret/   Cat 357
cotorrito   Mex 64
cotovía   Port + var totovía nonsp? or not distinguished? (1) 364
   [and 365]; (2) 366
críalo   off pop? 304
/cua de junc/   Cat 65
/— furxada/   [Cat gall de cua forcada] 151
/cucala/   Cat + ? (1) 396; (2) [399]
cuchareta   (1) pop 52; (2) pop 66
cucito   pop Andal + ? 403
cuclillo   pop 303
— común   bkn 303
— de Europa   bkn 303
— real   304
cuco   (1) off pop sp 303; (2) nonsp/fam 303-306 cuckoos; (3) pop
   sp 308, cf. cucu, cuquillo
(cuco) del moño   304
— moñón   pop 304
— piquigualdo   off 306
— piquinegro   off 305
— real   pop 304
cucu   var error? cuco (1) 303; (2) 308
cucua   (cucuá?, cf. Maj cucuiada) 364 [and 365?]
cucu (cuco?) del moño   pop 304
— (cuco?) real   pop 304

cuervo   (1) off pop 400; (2) nonsp/gen 397-400 crows; (3) conf? 399a
— de mar   var cuervo marino, cormorán 33
— marino   (1) pop nonsp/fam/gen 33-35 cormorants; (2) pop sp 33
— — moñudo   bkn 34
— merendero   398
cugujada   var cogujada 364 [and 365?]
cujada   var mispr? cugujada, cogujada 364, 365
cujaílla   pop Andal +? 358 (mispr? cajaílla)
culadera   pop Vizcaya 380a
[culapa   Ast "especie de troglodita" ?]
culebrera   pop Andal +? 135; v. águila culebrera
culiblanco   (1) pop nonsp? or conf? 463, 465, 468 wheatears; (2) pop
    Álava 380a; (3) [=totano 207? +?]
culirrojo   var colirrojo nonsp 473, 474 redstarts
culisca   pop Guipúzcoa 201
culo rubio   bkn 474
cuquillo   (1) pop Andal +? 308, cf. cuco (3); (2) var cuclillo 303;
    (3) pop reg 337 (?)
curita   510
[curro   Ast Leon kind of duck ?]
curruca   (1) pop nonsp 430, 433 + warblers (−); (2) off gen 428-440
— cabecinegra   off scl 436
— capirotada   off 431
— carrasqueña   off 437
— común   bkn 429
— de anteojo, c. de anteojos   bkn scl 438
— — cabeza negra   bkn scl 431
— — los jardines   bkn scl 429
[— — — pantanos   416? 417?]
— — pecho amarillo   bkn 423
— — Rüppell   off scl 435
— gavilán   bkn scl 428
— gavilana   off scl 428
— gris   bkn (1) 432; (2) 433
— mirlona   off 429
— mosquitera   off 430
— rabilarga   off 439
— sahariana   off 434
— sarda   off scl 440
— subalpina   bkn scl 437

curruca tomillera   off 438
— zarcera   off 432
— zarcerilla   off 433
curuca   var mispr? curuja 307
curuja   (1) pop? 307; (2) (coruja) 308

[dardabasí   "ave rapaz diurna" ?]
dendroica papinegra carigualda   off scl Eng 500
/denoiteira/   Port? nonsp? or not distinguished? 321, 322
desollador   (1) pop nonsp/gen 381, 383+ shrikes; (2) pop sp esp 383
— común   383
diablo   (1) pop Andal +? 20; (2) [=pájaro diablo 175?]
doradillo   (1) [377?]; (2) error, sense inappropriate 380a
dormitón   241
drena   495

eider   (1) off gen^2 81-84 eiders; (2) sp 82
eíder   var eider 82
eider común   bkn 82
— de Fischer   off scl 84
— — Steller   off scl 81
[eidero = eider]
eider real   off 83
elanio azul   off scl 127
elano   bkn scl 127
engañabobos   pop nonsp? or not distinguished? 321, 322 nightjars
engañamuchachos   245
engañapastor   (1) /?/ 314; (2) [Arag var engañapastores 321, 322];
    (3) [Nav = aguzanieves 390]
engañapastores   (1) pop nonsp? or not distinguished? 321, 322;
    (2) [= autillo 314?]; (3) [= pastorcillo de las aves   ?]
epecha   (1) 403; (2) [Nav = reyezuelo 451?, 452?]
[erismatura   bkn scl gen 85 +]
erismaturo leucocéfalo   bkn scl 85
escribano   (1) off pop nonsp/fam— 547-565+ buntings; (2) pop sp
    esp 550 and 555
— aureolado   off scl 560
— cabecinegro   off scl 562
— carirrojo   off scl 563

escribano cejigualdo off scl 558
— ceniciento off 554
— cerillo off 548
— cinereo off scl 553
— de Brandt off 551
— — Gmelin off 549
— enmascarado off 564
— herrumbroso off scl 561
— hortelano off 552
— lapón off scl 569
— montesino off 550
— nival off scl 570
— palustre off 565
— pigmeo off 557
— rústico off scl 559
— sahariano off 556
— soteño off 555
escribiente var escribano 555 + ?
escribiera var escribano 547, 555 + ?
escuatarola bkn scl 191
/esgrumador/ 545
esmerejón (1) off pop 143; (2) conf? /124/
espantadizo 471
[esparaván Arag = gavilán 122]
[esparvel var esparver 122]
esparver Cat Arag + ? 122
espátula (1) off pop 52; (2) bkn? scl 66; cf. cuchareta
— blanca bkn 52
— común bkn scl 66
espulgabueyes pop 44
esquilaso (esquilazo?) 391
estarna bkn? It 158
estarno var mispr? estarna 158
[estercolero var estercorario 246-249]
estercorario bkn scl gen/fam 246-249 skuas
— de cola larga (1) bkn scl 249; (2) error /246/
estornino (1) pop sp 388; (2) off gen 387-389 starlings
— común bkn 388
— negro off 389
— pinto off 388

estornino rosa   387
— rosado   off 387
estrellina   var mispr? estrelliña 452
estrelliña   pop Gal (cf. Port estrelinha) nonsp? or not distinguished?
    451, 452
estrige   bkn scl gen? improp? sp 307
[estrígido   bkn scl fam 307-320 owls]

faisán   (1) pop sp 160; (2) nonsp 160+ pheasants; (3) pop N Cast
    +? 152
— cantábrico   152
— chino de collar   Mex 160
— común   160
— de collar blanco   bkn 160
— vulgar   off 160
falaris   arch bkn Lat 175
falarópodo   bkn scl gen/fam 239-240 phalaropes
— de cuello rojo   bkn 240
— gris   bkn 239
falaropo   off scl gen/fam 239-240 phalaropes
— picofino   off 240
— picogrueso   off 239
— rojo   bkn 240
falcinelo brillante, falcinelo   bkn scl 53
[falcino   Arag "vencejo" 325? 352?]
fardela del Atlántico   mispr? pardela bkn 20
— — Mediterráneo   mispr? pardela bkn 24
ferre   Ast 124?
/ferreira/   NW, Port? 406 [but cf. Port ferreiro (1) 327; (2) = pe-
    dreiro, one of 348-352 (swallows); (3) = gaivão nonsp gulls]
flamenco   (1) off pop 54; (2) nonsp/fam flamingoes
— rosa   bkn 54
/flaveta/   480
florentina   pop reg Segovia +? 174
focha   (1) pop sp 175; (2) off pop nonsp/gen 175-176 coots
— común   off 175
— cornuda   off 176
foja   var focha 175 [and 176?]
fragata   (1) sp 36; (2) nonsp/gen/fam 36+ frigate-birds

frailecillo   (1) off pop 290;   (2) pop nonsp? conf? 185, 187 + ?
   ringed plovers; (3) /?/ 183; (4) /?/ 545
— común   off 290
francolín común   157
— de collar   157
— pequeño   pop Guipúzcoa 192
francolino   improp conf? 178 [157?]
frangüeso, franhueso   Ast 110
fringilago   bkn? 512
friolenco   438
/friorque/ apívoro   mispr? triorque apívoro 130 (cf. Greek triorkhes)
frisa, friso   pop Andal+ 62
fúlica   (1) bkn scl gen 175-176 coots; (2) bkn sp 175
— negra   bkn scl 175
fuligula, fulígula   bkn scl gen 69-72 pochards (—)
— de cresta   bkn 70
— — ojos blancos   bkn 72
— gris   bkn 69
— marila   bkn scl 69
— moñuda   bkn 70
fulmar   off 31
— europeo   bkn 31
— glacial   bkn scl 31
fumarel   off gen 267-269 terns (—), black terns (+) [cf. Cat fumarell,
   fumadell nonsp terns]
— aliblanco   off scl 268
— cariblanco   off 269
— común   off 267
fusca   bkn 79

gacha   var? agachadiza 196 + ?
— menor   198
gafarrón   conf nonsp? finches (1) pop Murcia + ? 535; (2) E? 528;
   (3) [Cat gafarró 529, 530]
galdón   var alcaudón 383, 385 + ? shrikes
galdona   var alcaudón 383 + ?
galerita   bkn? scl 364 [and 365?]
galfarro   Leon 122
gálgulo   (1) 392; (2) /?/ 386

gallareta   pop nonsp/gen 175-176 coots
— cornuda   176
— de mar   pop reg 282
gallarón   (1) m 177; (2) improp error 178; (3) [arch = /?/zancuda ?]
gallina ciega   pop nonsp? or not distinguished? 321, 322 nightjars
— de agua   175
— — río   174
— montés   153
— silvestre   bkn 151
— sorda   pop reg 199
gallineta   (1) pop 199; (2) pop 175
— ciega   199
gallito (de?) marzo   337; v. also gallo de marzo
gallo   /?/ (gallo de mar?) 282
— azul   pop Andal 171
— de bosque   pop N Cast 152; v. also pequeño gallo de bosque
— — cañar (/Cañar/)   pop Andal 171 (cf. Val gall de canyar)
— — mar   290
— — marzo   pop Andal +? 337
— — monte   (1) sp 152; (2) bkn fam 148-153 grouse
— lira   off 151
— montés   152
— silvestre   bkn 152
ganga   (1) pop sp 292; (2) nonsp 291-294 sandgrouse
— común   off 292
— del desierto   bkn 294
— de Pallas   off 294
— moteada   off 293
ganso   (1) pop nonsp 92-103 geese; (2) sp (not distinguished) 92, 95;
   v. also oca
— bravo   (1) pop sp esp 92, 95; (2) [nonsp, any "wild goose" 92-103]
— careto   bkn? 93
— ceniciento salvaje   bkn 92
— cenizo   bkn? 92
— cisnal   off scl 99
— de la mies   bkn? 95
— — las nieves   bkn? 97
— del Canadá   bkn and Mex 102
— de los percebes   bkn? 101
— frente blanca   Mex 93

ganso graznador   Mex 102

[— gris   nonsp/gen 92-96 grey geese]

— gritón   Mex 102

— monjita   bkn? 101

[— negro   nonsp/gen 100-103 black geese]

— peluquín   off 98

garceta   (1) off gen 41-42 egrets (—); (2) sp 41

— común   off 41

— grande   off 42

— menor   bkn 41

garcete   var garceta 41

garcilla   off gen 43-44

— bueyera   off 44

— cangrejera   off 43

gargantiazul   pop 480

gargantirrojo   476

/gargolet/   var mispr? Cat cargolet 403

garrapatera   pop 44

[garrapatero   44?]

garrapatosa   pop Andal + ? 44

garrapino, garrapinos   pop nonsp? or conf? 509, 512

garza   (1) pop nonsp/fam — herons (incl egrets); (2) off gen and pop
     nonsp esp 39-40 herons (—); (3) improp sp 43

— blanca   pop nonsp? not distinguished? 41, 42

— canaria   pop 43

— cangrejera   43

— ceniza   pop? 39

— común   bkn 39

— cristada   bkn 39

— de mar   Cat? 180 [cf. Cat garsa de mar 180]

— — noche   pop 45

— diablo   pop Andal + ? 53

— dorada   bkn? 48

— enana   46

— gris   (1) 39; (2) 45

— imperial   off 40

— mochuelo   pop reg 48

— moruna   pop Andal + ? 40

— pardilla   bkn 40

— purpúrea   bkn scl 40

garza real   off pop 39
— — cenicienta   bkn 39
— — purpúrea   bkn 40
— roja   bkn? 40
garzota   (1) nonsp/gen 41-42 egrets; (2) improp? sp 41
— común   bkn 41
— grande   bkn 42
gateador   W? (cf. Port gateador) var agateador 517, 518
gaudón   Álava 383
gavilán   (1) off pop sp 122; (2) off gen— 122-123; (3) pop Andal +?
   124; (4) improp? conf? 130
— común   bkn 122
— de las palomas   bkn scl 124
— — los gorriones   bkn 122
— griego   off 123
gavina   conf (1) pop reg var gaviota nonsp 250-266 gulls (cf. Cat gavina nonsp gulls); (2) pop reg smaller gulls and sp esp 266;
   (3) pop Andal +? 273 +? (cf. Port gavina nonsp terns)
/gavinot/   Cat (1) error /254/; (2) [251]
gavión   (1) off augm gaviota 251; (2) [Nav var avión = vencejo 325?
   327?]
— cabecinegro   off 257
gaviota   (1) off pop nonsp/fam— 250-266 gulls; (2) improp sp 251,
   253, 258, 259
— argéntea   off scl 253
— blanca   bkn 254
— cabecinegra   off scl 261
— cana   off scl 254
— común   (1) bkn 253; (2) bkn 263
— de Audouin   off scl 258
— — Bonaparte   off 260
— — cabeza negra   (1) bkn 261; (2) bkn 263
— — pies amarillos   bkn 252
— — Ross   off 264
— — Sabine   off 265
— — tres dedos   bkn scl 266
— enana   off 262
— gigante   bkn 251
— hiperbórea   off scl 255
— marfil   off scl 250

gaviota marina   bkn scl 251
— monja   275
— negra, g. oscura   bkn 252
— picofina   off 259
— polar   off 256
— reidora   bkn scl 263
— — común   off scl 263
— rosa   bkn scl 264
— sombría   off scl 252
— tridáctila   off scl 266
— turca   bkn 257
gaya   393
gayo   (1) arch? reg? 391 [cf. Port gaio 391]; (2) [Álava, Arag Nav = grajo ?]
gerifalco   var gerifalte 141
gerifalte   141
glareola de alas negras   bkn scl 244
glayo   Ast var gayo 391
godón   reg var alcaudón 381 +?
golleria (gollería?)   Cat? /?/ 380a
[golondra   Co Arag=alondra 367?]
golondrina   (1) pop nonsp fam 384-352 swallows and martins; (2) pop sp 350; (3) improp sp 352
— común   off 350
— dáurica   off scl 351
— de las rocas   bkn scl 349
— — — ventanas   pop? 352
— — mar   (1) pop nonsp fam— 267-281 terns; (2) improp sp 268, 269, 270, 271
— — — ártica   bkn 273
— — — chica   bkn 277
— — — común   bkn 272
— — — enana   bkn 277
— — — gigante   bkn 279 (but cf. 278)
— — — moñuda   bkn 279
— — — rosácea   bkn 274
— — ribera   pop 348
— — río   348
— — San Martín   348
— — ventana   pop? 352

golondrina roja   bkn 351
— silvestre   bkn 349
[golorito   Burgos Rioja = jilguero 533]
gorrión   (1) pop sp 520; (2) off pop fam 520-524 sparrows (and snow-finches)
— alpino   off 524
— campesino   bkn 523
— chillón   off 523
— común   off 520
— doméstico   bkn 520
— italiano   off 520a
— molinero   (1) off 522; (2) conf? 521
— montés   pop reg 523
— moruno   off pop 521
— serrano   pop 522
— triguero   bkn? 547
graja   (1) off 398; (2) pop nonsp or conf? 395, 396, 397, 399a
   crows (−); cf. chova and grajo
— cenicienta   bkn 399b
— de pico amarillo   bkn 396
— — — bermejo, g. de p. encarnado, g. de p. rojo   bkn 395
— menor   bkn 397
grajilla   (1) off 397; (2) nonsp? conf? 395, 399a +? crows (−)
grajillo   399a +?
grajo   pop nonsp? or conf? 391, 395, 396, 398, 399a, 400 crows;
   cf. chova and graja
— blanco   pop Andal +? 107
/gralha de pico vermelho/   Port /396/ [395]
gran cormorán   bkn 33
gran duque   bkn French 309
gran golondrina de mar   pop? Andal 272
grebul   mispr grébul 153
grébul   var grévol 153
grévol   (Cat grèvol) off 153
grigallo   (1) 151; (2) /152/
grúa   arch and Cat var grulla 162
grulla   (1) pop sp 162; (2) off pop nonsp/fam 162-164 cranes
— blanca   bkn 163
— cenicienta   bkn 162
— común   off 162

grulla coronada   bkn 162? 164?
— damisela   off 164
— de Numidia   bkn 164
— mora   pop 164
— moruna   pop Andal +? 164
— real   bkn 162
— siberiana blanca   off 163
guardarrío   pop reg W? (cf. Port guarda-rios) 333
[guarilla   Álava "especie de águila pequeña" ?]
güerequeque   pop Peru Ecuador +? 184
guerrero   pop Andal 512
guía de las codornices   pop Andal +? 170; v. also guión de codornices
— — — gallinetas   pop Andal +? 48
guillemote   bkn Eng Fr gen? 286 +?
guión de codornices   off pop 170
— — las codornices   var guión de codornices 170
[guirle   Sal = vencejo 325? 352?]
gulloria   arch 359
gurriato   (1) [young of 520]; (2) 520

halcón   (1) pop nonsp/gen 137-147 falcons; (2) pop sp esp 138
— abejero   off scl 130
— baharí   (1) off 138b; (2) [arch one of subsps of 138, 138b?]
   v. also baharí
— borní   off 139
— común   off 138
— coronado   131?
— de Eleonor   off scl 142
— gentil   138
— gerifalte   off 141
— lanario   139
— neblí   (1) 138 but esp 138a; (2) off 138a
— palumbario   bkn? 124?
— peregrino   bkn scl 138
— real   138
— sacre   off 140
— tagarote   (1) off 138c; (2) [arch one of subsps of 138, 138c?]
   v. also tagarote

halcón vespertino   bkn scl 144
halieto   bkn scl 136
harelda de los hielos   bkn scl 76; v. also havelda
harfango   bkn Swedish/French 310
— de las nieves   bkn 310
/havelda/   mispr for harelda (Icelandic?) off scl 76
hematópodo   bkn scl 180
herrerillo   (1) pop nonsp? or conf? 504, 509, 510, /?/ 512 tits (−);
   (2) pop sp esp 510
— capuchino   off 508
— ciáneo   off scl 511
— común   off 510
— — africano   off 510b
— — europeo   off 510a
— moñudo   bkn 508
herrero   338
herreroche   512
herreruelo   var herrerrillo 509 [510?]
hormiguero   pop 347
hortelano   (1) pop 552; (2) conf? [565] (v. hortolano)
hortolano   (1) var hortelano 552; (2) conf? 565
hubara   off 179
— canaria   off 179b
— mora   off 179a
huerequeque   pop Peru +? 184

[ibis   bkn fam− 53+ ibises]

jacaralla (jaracalla?)   367
jamas   /?/ 535
jaracalla (jacaralla?)   367
jarero   439
jilguera   f of jilguero 533
jilguerillo basto   529
jilguero   off pop 533
judía   pop Andal Arag Murcia Nav +? 183
junco pizarroso   off scl Eng 566

labanco var lavanco 91

[lagópedo var lagópodo 148+ grouse]

lagópodo off scl gen— 148-149 grouse (−)

— escandinavo off 148

— escocés off 149

/laro ridibundo/ scl 263

lavanco (1) pop Andal +? 91; (2) [Cuba 64]; (3) cf. somormujo
    lavanco 5

lavandera (1) pop sp 380a; (2) pop nonsp/gen 377-380 wagtails;
    (3) pop nonsp/gen— 207+ sandpipers; (4) improp? sp 207, 210;
    (5) [Port /?/ 187 +?]

— blanca off 380

— — común off 380a

— — enlutada off 380b

— boyera off 377

— — alemana off 377a

— — balcánica off 377g

— — de Sykes off 377b

— — escandinava off 377c

— — ibérica off 377e

— — inglesa off 377f

— — italiana off 377d

— cascadeña off 379

— cetrina off 378

— chica pop 210

— común 210

— real bkn? 377f

/laverca/ mispr (Port laverça) 367

lechuza (1) pop sp 307; (2) nonsp in compounds 307, 310-312,
    318-320 owls (−)

— campestre off 318

— común off 307

— de las peñas 318

— — monte pop? 318

— — Tengmalm off 320

— enana bkn 312

— gavilana off 311

— mora off 319

— serval bkn 310

lililo pop Andal 347

limicola pigmeo   bkn scl 234
[limícolo   bkn scl fam 196-236 waders (−)]
limosa   bkn scl gen 205-206 godwits
— egocéfala   bkn scl 205
— roja   bkn 206
linacero   pop Andal 555
liñacero   pop NW 535
/llansetina/   Cat? 366
locustela   bkn scl gen 409-414 grasshopper-warblers
— de carrizal   bkn 410
— fluvial   bkn scl 411
— manchada   bkn 413
lubano, lúbano, lugano   pop var lúgano 532
lúgano   off pop 532

malvasia   mispr? malvasía 85
malvasía   off pop 85
/malvis/   orthog error malvís 493
malvís   pop 493
— alirrojo   bkn 493
— cantábrico   bkn 494
malviz   m var malvís 493
mancón   pop Andal + ? 175
— azul   pop Andal + ? 171
maquetes   bkn scl 236
/margaso/   [Cat margassa, margassó 385] 385
marica   pop 393
— común   393
marismeña   358
martín cazador   pop reg 333
— del río   45
martinete   (1) off pop 45 ; (2) /?/ 327
martín peña   45
— pescador   (1) off pop sp 333 ; (2) nonsp fam 331-333 kingfishers
— — alción   off 332
— — pío   off 331
— zambullidor   pop reg 333
mataperros   pop nonsp/gen^3 165-170 crakes and rails
matinero   565

medio chorlito /?/ 194
meleón   var mispr? melión 119
melión   conf? (1) 119; (2) Andal 135; (3) /128/
menseja   pop Álava Nav 512
mergánsar   bkn gen 33 + cormorants; v. mergo (1)
mergo   (1) bkn scl fam/gen 33-35 cormorants; (2) improp sp 33;
    (3) bkn scl pop? Mex gen 86-89 mergansers; (4) improp sp 88
— americano   Mex 88
— copetón   Mex 87
— de caperuza   Mex 86
— — cresta   bkn 87
— — pecho oscuro   Mex 87
mérgulo   (1) bkn scl gen³ 284, 288, 289 auks (−), auklets (+); (2) bkn
    sp 284
— crestado   off 289
— lorito   off 288
— marino   off 284
merla, mielra, mierla   reg var mirlo 491
milano   (1) off pop nonsp/gen 125-126 kites; (2) pop sp 125; (3) pop
    conf? improp? sp 131, cf. milano blanco, nonsp? 131-134 harriers;
    (4) error? 124, but cf. milano jaspeado, nonsp? 122-124 hawks
— blanco, m. gris   132
— jaspeado   pop Andal 122
— negro   off pop 126
— real   off pop 125
— rojo   125
mileón   var mispr? melión 119
millero   pop Andal + ? 527
miloca   [Cat 320] (1) 318 (?); (2) 320
[miloje   Sal = buitre 108?]
mirla   var mirlo 491
mirlo   (1) pop sp 491; (2) with qualifier, 402, 471, 490 other passerines
    esp thrushes
— acuático   off 402
— collarizo   off 490
— — nórdico   off 490a
— — serrano   off 490b
— común   off 491
— de agua   bkn 402
— pintado   pop? 471

mito off pop 503

mochete 146

mochuelo (1) pop sp 313; (2) nonsp, with qualifiers, 312, 313, 320
  owls (−); (3) improp sp 312

— chico off 312

— común off 313

— de Tengmalm bkn 320

— vulgar bkn 313

mohino pop 392

— rabilargo 392

molinero (1) /?/ 521 [522?]; (2) conf? 565

mondra de mar pop reg 230

monigero (boñiguero?) pop Andal +? 107

montañés pop Andal +? 527

moñudo pop? 70

/morell/ Cat /70/ [77]

/— capellut/ Cat 70

/— de mar/ Cat 77

morinelo bkn scl 194

morito off pop 53

mormón 290

/moscaret/ Cat? 422 +?

moscareta E? nonsp? subfam? 454, 458 flycatchers

— de collar bkn 455

moscón 519; v. pájaro moscón

— de cola larga bkn 503

mosqueta (1) improp sp 444; (2) [nonsp/gen+ warblers (−)]

mosquilla pop Andal nonsp? not distinguished? 441, 442

mosquitera var mispr? mosquitero 441

mosquitero (1) off pop nonsp/gen 441-450 warblers (−); (2) pop
  nonsp 458+ flycatchers

— bilistado off 447

— boreal off scl 449

— común (1) off 442; (2) bkn 441

— de Bonelli bkn 443

— — Pallas off 448

— — Schwarz off scl 446

— moruno bkn 443

— musical off 441

— papialbo off 443

mosquitero pardo   bkn 442
— silbador   off scl 444
— sombrío   off scl 445
— troquiloide   off scl 450
— verde   bkn 444
motacila   bkn scl improp sp 380a [gen 377-380 wagtails]
motolita   /?/ 380a
muscaria   bkn 458 [454-459? flycatchers]
muscicapa, muscícapa   bkn scl 458 [454-459? flycatchers]

neblí   138 but esp 138a; v. also halcón neblí
[negrera   Andal "especie de pato salvaje", negreta? 77-79]
negreta   (1) nonsp? 77 and 79 scoters; (2) error? 70
— de alas blancas   Mex 77
— — marejada   Mex 78
negrete   pop 72
negrón   off gen 77-79 scoters
— careto   off 78
— común   off 79
— de Steller   bkn 81
— especulado   off 77
nevadilla   var Andal +? nevatilla nonsp? 377, 377f +?
nevatilla   (1) pop nonsp/gen 377-380 wagtails; (2) sp esp 380a
— citrina   bkn scl 378
— de los arroyos blanca   bkn 380a
— gris   bkn 379
nevera   183
nevereta   380a
nictea alba   bkn scl 310
nictícorax   bkn scl 45
niotilta varia   off scl 501
niso común   bkn scl 122
noveleta   bkn Cat? gen? [5-9] grebes
— cuellinegra   bkn 8
— cuellirroja   bkn 7
nucifraga, nucífraga   bkn scl 394
[nuétiga   Sant = lechuza 307?]

oca   (1) f of ganso; (2) pop nonsp 92-103 geese; (3) sp 95 [and 92? cf. ganso]

— asiática   bkn /99/ (not Asiatic species)

— cenicienta   bkn? 92

— — salvaje   bkn 92

— de frente blanca   bkn scl 93

— del Canadá   bkn and Mex 102

— de pico corto   bkn scl 96

— salvaje   Mex 93

— silvestre   95

/oliva/   [Cat òliba] 307

[olivarcero   Nav "cierto pajarillo" ?]

[ollera   = herrerillo 510?]

oncejo   var vencejo 325 + ?

[/oreneta/], /oroneta/   Cat Val 350

oropéndola   off pop 386

ortega   off pop 291

osífraga, osífrago   bkn scl 110

ostrero   (1) off pop 180; (2) nonsp/fam 180 + oystercatchers

— común   off 180a

— unicolor   off 180b

oto   (1) bkn scl (*Otus*) /314/ [317]; (2) bkn scl (*Otis*) 177

/oureol/   ? 386

págalo   (euphemism for cágalo) off gen/fam 246-249 skuas

— grande   off 247

— parasítico   off scl 246

— parásito   bkn scl 246

— pomarino   off scl 248

— rabero   off 249

pagañera   pop reg Sal + ? 322 [and 321?]

pagaza   off gen^2 270-271 terns (−)

— piconegra   off 270

— piquirroja   off 271

paino   var? mispr? paiño pop improp? sp 267; v. also paiño

— mayor   pop? 269

paíño, paiño   (1) off nonsp/gen^3 15-19 petrels [cf. Port painho, 15-29? petrels and shearwaters]; (2) (paino) nonsp? terns (± ?)

— común   off 18

paiño de Leach   off 16
— — Madeira   off 17
— — Wilson   off 15
— pechialbo   off 19
pajaraco   /?/   pop Andal 108
pajarel   nonsp? conf? 534, 535
pajarita de las nieves   pop 380a
pájaro arañero   pop? 516; v. also arañero
— bobo   (1) /1/; (2) [nonsp *Spheniscidae*, penguins]
— burro   36
[— camacho   = pardillo 535]
— carpintero   338
— diablo   175; v. also diablo
— gato   off pop Am 407
— linero   536 [535?]
— loco   472
— moscón   off pop 519
— negro   /?/ 468
— polilla   pop reg 333
— rojo   /?/ 470
— solitario   472
— tonto   var ave tonta nonsp 547+ buntings
— toro   pop Andal var avetoro 48
[— trapaza   ?]
paleta, paleto   pop Andal +? 52
paletón   (1) pop 66; (2) pop 52; cf. cuchareta
palmera   pop Andal 436
paloma   off pop nonsp/gen 295-299 pigeons and doves
— brava   (1) pop Andal +? 296; (2) bkn 295
— bravía   off 296
— de collar   bkn 297
[— — Groenlandia   one of auks, 284?]
— del Cabo   off Eng 30
— montés   296
— rabiche   off 299
— roquiza   bkn 296
— silvestre   conf (1) nonsp, any wild pigeon; (2) improp? sp 295, 296, 297
— torcaz   off pop 297
— turque   off 298

paloma zorita, p. zura, p. zurana   var paloma zurita 295, 296
— zurita   conf? not distinguished? (1) off pop? 295; (2) pop 296
— zurra   var paloma zurita 296 [and 295?]
papafigo   (1) (also Port) 386; (2) pop /?/ 431 [430?]; (3) [= papa-
    moscas 454-459 flycatchers] Note conf of papafigo (cowl) and papafi-
    go (fig-eater), so that inappropriate names of becafigo, picafigo(s) are
    given to 430, 431?, 454-459
papahigo   (1) 386; (2) 430
papamoscas   (1) off pop subfam/gen² 454-459 flycatchers; (2) pop sp
    esp 458; (3) improp sp 455
— cerrojillo   off 454
— collarino   off 455
— de collar   bkn 455
— gris   off 458
— luctuosa   bkn 454
— narciso   off scl 456
— papirrojo   off 457
— pardo   off 459
papavientos   pop nonsp? or not distinguished? 321, 322 nightjars
papicolorado, papirrojo, paporrubio   reg var petirrojo 476
pardal   (1) reg 535; (2) reg? (Cat Port) 520
/pardal de bardissa/   Cat 406
pardela   off gen 20-25 shearwaters
— capirotada   off 23
— cenicienta   off 24
— chica   off 21
— de Audubon   off 22
— pichoneta   off 20
— — balear   off 20c
— — inglesa   off 20a
— — yelkouan   off scl 20b
— sombría   off 25
pardilla   (1) pop 58 (cerceta pardilla); (2) 158 (perdiz pardilla); (3) var
    pardillo 535
pardillo   (1) pop sp 535; (2) off gen 534-537; (3) var pardilla 158
— común   off 535
— de Hornemann   off scl 537
— piquigualdo   off scl 534
— sizerín   off 536 (cf. French sizerin 536)
[pardón   Ast falcon ?]

pardote   pop 72
parlanchín   433
paro   bkn Lat gen 504-512 tits
— azul   bkn 510
— carbonero, p. mayor   bkn 512
— moñudo   bkn 508
— rabilargo   bkn 503
parpar   476
[parpayega, parpayuela   Ast = codorniz 159]
parro   55
parula americana   off scl 499
/pasera de las rojes/   [Cat pàssera de les roques, p. de les roges 471] 471
pastorcilla   432
[pastorcillo de las aves   ?]
patera   pop Andal +? 52
patiblanca   148
patín   20
patiseco   476
patito   57
pato   (1) pop nonsp 55-85 ducks; (2) sp esp 55
— arlequín   off 80
— bocón   Mex (1) 66; (2) 69
— boludo   Mex 69
[— buceador   bkn nonsp 68-75 diving ducks]
— cabezón   Mex 62
— calvo   Mex 64
— canelo   pop 91
— careta   mispr? careto 65
— careto   pop Andal +? 65
— castellano   62
— chalcuán   Mex 64
— chillón jorobado   Mex 75
— — ojos dorados   bkn? Mex 73
— chiquito   56
— colorado   off 68
— común   Mex 55
— cuaresmeño   Mex 66
— cuchara   off 66
— cuchareta   pop 66
— cucharetero   66

pato cucharón, p. cucharudo   Mex 66
— de collar   Mex 55
— — flojel   82
[— — ojos blancos   72?]
— — sierra   pop Andal + ? improp? sp 87 (+ ? mergansers); v. also
   pato sierra 88
— franciscano   pop Andal + ? 63
— galán   Mex 55
— golondrino (golondrina?)   Mex 65
— jaspeado   58
— mandarín   off bkn 67
[— marino   bkn nonsp 76-84 sea-ducks]
— monja   Mex 75
[— nadador   bkn nonsp/gen+ 55-67 surface-feeding ducks]
— negro   (1) pop 79; (2) /?/ 77
— panadero   Mex 64
— pardo de grupo   bkn? Mex 62
— pelucón   bkn? 70
— pescuecilargo   bkn 65
— pinto   Mex 62
— porrón   pop 85; v. also porrón
— rabilargo   bkn? 65
— rabudo   pop 65
— rampla   Mex 86
— real   pop 55
— — de mar   bkn? 63
— serrano   57
— sierra   (pato de sierra?) 88 [and 87?]
— silbador   63
[— silbón   63]
— silvestre   bkn? 55
— tarro   (1) pop nonsp/gen 90-91 sheld-ducks; (2) sp esp 90;
   (3) /?/ 85
paviota   var gaviota 253+ gulls
[pavo del río, p. marino   236?]
pazpallá   159
pechel   476
pechiazul   off pop 480
— medalla blanca   off 480a
— — roja   off 480b

pechiblanco   pop 402

pechicolorado, pechirrojo   (1) var petirrojo 476; (2) 535

pechirrubio   var petirrojo 476

/pedreo/   mispr pedrero 468

pedrero   pop Andal +? 468

pega   (1) Gal 391; (2) reg? (Port) 393

— reborda   383 +? (cf. pegarrebordas) shrikes?

— rebordada   (1) /?/ 391; (2) [381-385?]

pegarrebordas   pop reg 385 +? (cf. pega reborda) shrikes?

pelarrocas   /?/ [Cat pela-roques 516] 516

pelicano   var pelícano 37 +

pelícano   (1) sp 37; (2) nonsp/fam 37-38 + pelicans

— ceñudo   off 38

— común   bkn 37

— vulgar   off 37

pelidna   bkn scl gen 223+ stints (+)

— cocorlí   bkn 231

— de los Alpes   bkn scl 230

— — Temminck   bkn scl 225

— enana   bkn scl 223

pella   (1) Andal + ? var arpella 119; (2) [Sant "ave de rapiña" 119?];
   (3) 39

peñasca   463

peñato   525

[peñerina   Ast = cernícalo 146?]

pepita   var (mispr? pezpita) pizpita 380a

pequeño gallo de bosque   bkn 151

percha   403

perdicero   pop Cast +? 117

perdiz   (1) pop nonsp various smaller members of order *Galliformes*,
   148-160 game-birds (−), grouse and partridges; (2) off gen² 154-
   156, 158 partridges; (3) pop sp esp 156; (4) improp sp 158;
   (5) with qualifiers 243 pratincole

— blanca   150

— blancal   148

— cenicienta   bkn 158

— chocha   var error? chocha perdiz 199

— común   off 156

— de las arenas   243

— — — rocas   bkn 154

perdiz de mar   pop reg 243
— griega   off scl 154
— gris   158
— mora   155
— moruna   off 155
— nival   off 150
— pardilla   off 158
— patiblanca   148
— real, p. roja   156
pernetero   pop Andal + ? 107
petirrojo   off pop 476
[peto   Ast = pico, picamaderos 338 + ?]
petrel   (1) pop nonsp 15-18 storm-petrels;   (2) off gen 26-29 petrels;
    (3) improp sp 15, 18
— aliblanco   off 28
— de Bulwer   off 26
— — Kermadec   off 27
— diablotín   off 29
pezpita, pezpítalo   var pizpita 380a
picabuey   388 (but cf. picabueyes 44)
picabueyes   pop 44
picafigo   (1) 386;   (2) 431;   v. papafigo
picafigos   (1) [386?];   (2) 430 [431?];   v. papafigo
picagrega   383
picamaderos   nonsp? 338, 340
[picanza   Sal = picaza 393]
picanzo   v. alcaudón picanzo 385
picapinos   340
picaposte   338
picapotros   pop Álava 340
picapuerco   nonsp? conf? 343, 344
picapuertas dorsiblanco   bkn 342
— mayor   bkn 340
— menor   bkn 343
picaraza   var picaza 393
picarrelincho   (1) 338 cf. pitorrelincho;   (2) error? 380a
pica rústica   bkn scl 393
picatocino   343
[picatroncos   (1) Rioja = pájaro carpintero, nonsp? 338 + ? wood-
    peckers;   (2) Nav passerine ?]

picaza   393
— chillona, p. manchada   383
— marina   (1) /54/ sense inexplicable;   (2) [70? cf. Port pêga do mar 70]
picharchar   pop Vizcaya 460
pico   (1) pop nonsp/fam— 338-346 woodpeckers;   (2) sp esp 338;
   (3) off in compounds used for smaller woodpeckers 340-345 (pito for larger)
— alazán   pop? 340
— barreno   338
— carpintero   nonsp? 338, 340
— — negro   bkn 346
— ceniciento   bkn 339
— cruzado   pop var piquituerto 543
— dorsiblanco   off scl 342
pico duro   541
picofino   408
pico gordo, picogordo   off pop 546
picoideo tridáctilo   bkn scl 345
pico leuconoto   bkn scl 342
— mayor   bkn? scl 340
— mediano   off scl 344
— menor   off scl 343
— negro   346
— picapinos   off 340
— real   338
[picorrelinche   Burgos Sant = pico verde 338, cf. pitorrelincho]
picorro   338
pico sirio   off scl 341
picotero de Europa, p. vulgar   bkn 401
picotijera   (1) error? 267;   (2) [Am nonsp/fam *Rynchopidae* skimmers]
pico tridáctilo   off scl 345
pico-tuerto   pop var piquituerto 543
pico verde   338
picuda   (1) [199?];   (2) /?/ 196
[picudilla   199?]
pigargo   (1) off scl sp 128;   (2) off gen 128-129 sea-eagles;   (3) conf? 136
— cabeciblanco   bkn 129

pigargo común   bkn 128
— de Pallas   bkn 129
pilato   pop Andal + ? 52
pildoré   pop Vizcaya 192
pillera   195
pilotero   pop Andal 130
/pimpím/   v. pimpín 525
pimpín   pop Gal 525 [but Port pimpim /?/ one of *Parinae* 504-512,
   tits]
pinchahigos   /?/ 426, but cf. papafigo, picafigo(s)
pinche   525
pinchón   var pinzón 525
pingüino   (1) *283 (first bird to which name "penguin" applied);
   (2) pop nonsp 282-283, 285-287 auks (incl guillemots); (3) error
   /1/; (4) [Gallicism for pájaro bobo penguins]
— gigante   *283
[pintacilgos], pintacilgo   NW? [Port pintassilgo 533] 533
pintadillo   533
[pintarrojo   Gal = pardillo 535?]
pinzoleta   pop Murcia + ? nonsp? conf? 421, 429, 431 warblers (−)
pinzoletica   pop Murcia + ? nonsp? conf? 439, 441, 442, 447
   warblers (−)
pizoletita   var mispr? pinzoletica 441 + ?
pinzón   (1) pop sp 525; (2) off gen/subfam 525-527 chaffinches;
   (3) improp sp 527
— común   off 525a
— del Teide   off scl 526
— real   (1) off pop 527; (2) 545; (3) 546
— vulgar   off 525
— — tintillón   off 525b
piñata   (1) pop 458; (2) 429 + ?; (3) 465 + ?
piñonero   (1) pop 546; (2) conf? 545; (3) /527/
pío   (1) pop reg Sant + ? 230; (2) [Sant /?/ 195]
piornero   pop Cast 463
pipi   var mispr? pipí 374
pipí   (1) pop nonsp/gen 369+ pipits; (2) improp? sp or sp esp 374
— cervino   bkn scl 375
— de los campos   bkn? scl 369
— — — prados   bkn? scl 374
pipita   Andal 380a

pipo   343

piquituerto   (1) pop sp 543; (2) off gen 542-544 crossbills
— común   off 543
— de fajas blancas   bkn 544
— — los abetos   bkn 541
— franjeado   off 544
— lorito   off scl 542
piroftalmo de cabeza negra   bkn scl 436
pisco   pop Gal Port 476
pispita   pop Andal var pizpita (1) nonsp/gen 377-380 wagtails; (2) sp
   esp 380a
— amarilla   pop 377
pitaciega   pop 321 [and 322?]
pitillo   pop reg 231
pitirrojo   (1) var petirrojo 476; (2) [=pardillo 535, cf. pechirrojo]
pito   (1) pop nonsp/fam— 338-346 woodpeckers; (2) off in compounds
   used for larger woodpeckers, 338, 339, 346
pitobarrenos   338; v. also pico barreno
pito cano   off scl 339
— negro   off 346
— real   (1) off pop 338; (2) pop Andal conf? 340
pitorra   199
pitorrelincho   338
pitorro   285 (but cf. pitorra 199, potorra 282)
pit-pit   pop nonsp/gen? 371, 374 pipits
pitrulín   366
píulo   /?/ 63
pizpita   pop nonsp/gen (cf. pispita) 377-380 wagtails
pizpitillo   var pizpita 380
platalea   (1) bkn scl 52; (2) error? 37
plectrófano de las nieves   bkn scl 570
pluvial   (1) bkn scl gen 185+ plovers (−); (2) off gen 242
— de collar interrumpido   bkn 187
— dorado   bkn 192
— egipcio   off 242
— gris   bkn 191
— pequeño   bkn 186
polla   174
— de agua   (1) off pop 174; (2) pop Andal +? nonsp/gen 166-168
   crakes; (3) conf? 175; (4) /170/ sense inappropriate

polla de agua Baillon bkn 167

— — — porzana bkn scl 166

pollo de agua pop Andal + ? nonsp/gen 166-168 crakes

polluela (1) pop nonsp 165-168 crakes and rails (−); (2) improp sp, or not distinguished? 165, 166, 167, 168; (3) off gen 166-169 crakes (−)

— bastarda off 168

— chica off 167

— común bkn 166

— de la Carolina off scl 169

— pequeña bkn scl 168

— pintoja off 166

— rubia pop Andal + ? 170

porrón (1) pop Andal 85; (2) off nonsp/gen^2 69-75

— albeola off scl 75

— bastardo off 69

— común off 71

— islándico off scl 74

— moñudo off 70

— osculado off 73

— pardo off 72

potorra, potorro pop Guipúzcoa 282

potrilla, potrito pop reg 338

/primavera/ Cat /?/ 510 [Cat primavera (1) 463; (2) 237]

/primavera petita/ Cat 509

primilla (1) pop 145; (2) Andal conf? 146; (3) improp? 122

primita var primilla 145

[procelaria, procelario bkn scl gen 20-25 shearwaters]

/ptarmigan/ Eng 150

pufino de los ingleses bkn scl 20

pulverilla 431

purgabueyes Andal var espulgabueyes 44

quebrantahuesos (1) off pop 110; (2) Andal reg, where 110 absent, 107; (3) bkn? gen 128-129 sea-eagles; (4) bkn? improp? sp 128; (5) conf? with 128 (cf. pigargo), /?/ 136

— de cabeza blanca bkn 129

quebrantón 110

quinceta, quincineta 183

quivevive pop Andal 512

rabiblanca   pop 463
rabicandil   pop Álava 380a
rabihorcado   (1) pop Am sp 36; (2) off pop Am nonsp/fam 36+
    frigate-birds
— común   bkn 36
— grande   off 36
rabilarga   pop Álava 380a
rabilargo   sundry birds with long tails (1) off pop 392; (2) pop reg
    65; (3) 503; (4) /?/ 238
rabirrojo   474
rabitojo   off 330
rabudo   pop Andal +? 65
raitán   pop Asturias 476
[raitana   Ast = petirrojo 476]
[raitín   Sant = petirrojo 476]
ralo acuático   (1) bkn scl 165; (2) /175/
/rapiña/   (not "name"?) 131
rascón   (1) off pop 165; (2) improp? without qualifier 170; (3) /175/
— de agua   pop 165
— — los prados   bkn? 170
— — retama   bkn 170
ratilla   pop Andal +? 403
ratonero   off gen 119-121 buzzards
— calzado   off 120
— común   off 119
— moro   off 121
— rubio   off 119a
rayuelo   196 +?
rebiruelo   348
redolín   pop 191
régulo   bkn scl 451 [and 452?]
rejilero   (1) pop Andal +? 107; (2) improp? (cf. boñiguero) 109
rendaja, rendajo   var arrendajo 391
revuelvepiedras   pop 195
rey de codornices   pop 170
— — las codornices   var rey de codornices 170
— — zarza   403
/reyet/   E? 452 [and 451?] [Cat reiet, reietó (1) 451, 452; (2) 333;
    (3) 408]

10

reyezuelo   (1) pop nonsp? or not distinguished? 451, 452; (2) off gen
   451-452 goldcrests
— listado   off 452
— sencillo   off 451
— — genuino   off 451a
— — tinerfeño   off scl 452a
reznero   pop? 44
robín americano   off Eng 496
rolla   Zamora 300
/roncadell/   Cat 59
roquero   off gen 471-472 rock-thrushes
— rojo   off 471
— solitario   off 472
roseta   /?/ Cat? 58
/rotget/   (Cat roget) 72
rubita   pop 470
ruhilla   pop reg 58
ruiblanca   pop nonsp 463, 465, 468 wheatears; cf. collalba, culiblanco,
   sacristán
[ruín   Álava = reyezuelo 451? 452?]
ruipego   pop reg 392
ruiseñor   (1) pop sp 477; (2) off gen— 477-479; (3) /?/ 531
— bastardo   off 408
— caliope   off scl 479
— común   off 477
— grande, r. mayor   bkn 478
— ruso   off 478
— silvestre   bkn 417

sabubilla   Andal var abubilla 337
sacre   arch /146/ [140]
sacristán   (1) pop sp 468; (2) improp? 465; cf. collalba, culiblanco,
   ruiblanca
salseno   Mex 57
/salta marges/   417 [Cat saltamarges 416? 417?]
saltamimbres   416
salteador   pop? nonsp/gen/fam 247, 248+ skuas
[sanantona   Sal = aguzanieves 380a]
/sanderling/   Eng 233

saradillo   Mex 64

sarapico   var zarapito 201+ curlews

sarceta   var Andal +? cerceta 57 [but Port sarzeta 198]

sardinero   pop 66

sarseruelo   (zarzeruelo? cf. zarcerillo) pop Andal +? 205

/sarset/   Cat reg Tarragona 57

serín   (1) bkn scl sp 529; (2) off gen— 529-530; (3) bkn improp sp
530

— canario   off 530

— verdecillo   off 529

serpentario   135

serrano   pop 404

serrata   mispr? serreta 87

serratilla   bkn? 89

serreta   off gen 86-89 mergansers [Cat Val serreta sp 87]

— cabezona   off 86

— chica   off 89

— grande   off 88

— mediana   off 87

/sibert/   (Cat Val sivert) 68

sietearreldes   460

sietecolores   pop Burgos Palencia + ? 533

silbón   pop 63

— real   pop reg 62

silguero   var jilguero 533

silvarronco   477

sirguero   var jilguero 533

[sisella   Arag = paloma torcaz 297]

sisón   off pop 178

sita europea   bkn scl 513

/sivert/   Cat 68

/skua/   (1) Eng scl 247; (2) Eng improp sp 248

sobrestante   476

soldadito   pop reg 533

(soldía, soldilla?), /soldiya/   pop Andal 480

solitaria   /?/ 474

solitario   pop 472

— azul   bkn 472

— de las rocas   bkn 471

somorgujo   var somormujo improp sp 5, 8

[somorgujón   var somormujo]

somormujo   (1) nonsp/gen/fam 5-9 grebes; (2) off gen— applied to two larger species 5, 6; (3) improp sp 5, 8?

— castaño   bkn 9

— cuellirrojo   off scl 6

— de cuello negro   bkn 8

— — mejillas grises   bkn 6

— lavanco   off 5

— menor   bkn 9

— moñudo   bkn scl 5

— orejudo   bkn scl 7

— pequeño   bkn 9

sorda   (1) pop nonsp 196+ (cf. agachadiza sorda) snipe; (2) 199

[sordilla   Andal "parecido a la alondra" ?]

[subigüela   Sal = alondra 367?]

[sucinda   Sal = alondra 367?]

sula loca   bkn /?/ 32

surnia ulula   bkn scl 311

surnio gavilán   bkn 311

[tadorna   Sant/ = cernícalo 146/]

— común   bkn scl 90

— de Belon   bkn scl (and cf. French tadorne de Belon) 90

tagarote   (1) 138c; (2) conf /138b/; (3) error? /143/; (4) [Port 137]

tarabilla   off gen 460-462 chats

— canaria   off 461

— común   (1) off 462; (2) bkn 460

— de collar   bkn 462

— norteña   off 460

/tarrarol/ Cat? 357

tarro   off gen 90-91 sheld-ducks

— blanco   off 90

— canelo   off 91

/tayaret/   (Cat tallaret) 422

tero, terutero, teruteru   pop Am 184

terrera   (1) pop sp 357; (2) off gen^2 353-354, 357-358 larks (−); (3) pop 367

— común   off 357

— de Franklin   off 354

terrera marismeña   off 358; v. also marismeña
— sahariana   off 353
terrerilla   pop var terrera 357 [and 367?]
terrerita   225
/terrerola/   Cat 367 [Cat terrerola (1) 367; (2) 357 (cf. terrera)]
/terreroli/   (Cat terrerolí) 357
terreruela   pop var terrera (1) 357; (2) 367
tetrao común   bkn scl 152
/thalassidroma leucorrhoa/   scl 16
/— oceanica/   scl 15
tintín   (1) pop reg 453; (2) pop reg 525
— bolsicón   pop Murcia +? 453
tintorero   pop Andal +? 473
tinúnculo   bkn scl 146
/titella/   Cat /367/ [374]
[toquillo, toquilo   Nav=picamaderos nonsp?]
torcaza, torcazo   297
torcecuello   off pop 347
[tordancha   (1) Nav=estornino 388; (2) "especie de tordo" ?]
tordella   489 [cf. Port tordeia 489]
tordilla   374 [and 376? cf. tordino]
tordino   376 [and 374? cf. tordilla]
tordo   (1) pop nonsp/gen 387-389 starlings; (2) pop sp esp 389;
   (3) bkn Lat gen 485-496 thrushes; (4) bkn improp? sp 494, 495
— alirrojo   bkn 493
— campanero   389 (but conf? tordo de campanario 388)
— castellano   pop Gal 489
— común   bkn 494
— de agua   pop 402
— — campanario   pop Navarre 388 (but conf? tordo campanero 389)
— — Castilla   pop Vizcaya 388
— — las rocas   bkn 471
— loco   bkn? 472
— mayor   bkn 495
— músico   bkn scl 494
— pardo   bkn 494
— real   bkn 495
— serrano   389
— solitario   389
torillo   off pop 161

torrondana /?/ (Cat torrodana) 367

tórtola (1) pop sp 300; (2) off gen 300-302 turtle-doves

— común off 300

— de collar bkn 301

— oriental off scl 302

— turca off 301

tótano var mispr? totano 207+

totano bkn scl gen 207+ sandpipers (±)

— de los ríos bkn 207

— — patas rojas bkn 212

— grande bkn 214

— solitario bkn scl 209

— verde bkn 207

totovía (1) off pop? 366; (2) pop nonsp? or not distinguished? 364, 365 short-toed larks

(— copetuda) 364

tova pop reg 364 [and 365?]

trepador (1) off gen/subfam 513-515 nuthatches; (2) bkn gen/fam 517-518 tree-creepers

— azul off 513

— corso off 514

— familiar bkn scl 517

— rupestre off 515

trepajuncos (1) 416; (2) /493/; cf arandillo

treparriscos off 516

trepatorres /?/ sense inappropriate 453

trepatroncos various tree-climbing birds (1) pop 513; (2) pop nonsp? or not distinguished? 517, 518; (3) 510

— de Europa bkn 513

triguera /?/ sense inappropiate 525

triguero (1) off pop 547; (2) pop Álava 381, error? etym inexplicable

— común bkn 547

tringa gris bkn scl 221

(triorque) apívoro bkn scl 130

troglodita m bkn Lat 403

troglodito (troglodita?) pequeño bkn scl 403

[trullo (1) pop Leon 57; (2) some other species of duck ?]

tumanavilla pop Andal 453

turra Soria +? var churra 291

tutuvía var totovía 364, 365

úlula   bkn 314
upupa   bkn? scl 337
uria   var mispr? uría 286+
uría   bkn scl gen 285-287 guillemots
— común   bkn 285
— de alas blancas   bkn 287
— lomvia   bkn scl 286
urogallo   off scl 152
urraca   off pop 393

/valona/   Cat 208
vanelo   bkn scl 183
vaqueruela   237
[vejeta   = cogujada 364? 365?]
vencejillo   pop 349
vencejo   (1) off pop nonsp/fam 325-330 swifts;   (2) pop sp esp 325;
   (3) improp sp 327;   (4) pop 352 (cf. avión)
— alpino   bkn scl 327
— común   off 325
— culiblanco   off 328
— pálido   off scl 326
— real   off 327
— unicolor   off scl 329
/verdaula/   552 [Cat (1) various buntings, sp esp 555;   (2) W Cat 548;
   (3) Majorca 552]
verdecillo   (1) pop 529;   (2) verbal conf with verderón 531
[verdel   Nav = verderón 531?]
verderol   (1) var verderón 531;   (2) /?/ 548
[verderolo   Ast var verderón]
verderón   (1) pop 531;   (2) improp? conf? 532;   (3) /?/ 548;   (4) bkn?
   gen? with qualifiers 548, 550, 555 +? buntings
(— cicí)   555 cf. cip-cip
— común   off 531
— de seto   bkn 548
— — vallado   bkn 555
— loco   550
— serrano   off 528
— /zizí/ (cicí)   555 cf. cip-cip
verdezuelo   531
verdón   var verderón   531

[verdonce   Andal var verderón]
verdoncillo   pop 528
verdugo   nonsp? 383 +? shrikes (cf. desollador)
vilano   var? milano (1) 125; (2) /?/ 122
viñadera   Andal 470
viñera   426
vireo   (1) off scl gen 502+   vireos; (2) /?/ 386
víreo, [virio   = oropéndola] 386
vireo aceitunado   bkn 502
— ojirrojo   off 502
vuelvepiedras   (1) off pop 195; (2) Andal 180

/xibeca/   Cat 314
/xirlu/   (Cat xirlo) 367
/xurra/   Cat 291 cf. churra [Cat also 292]

zambullidor   pop? improp? sp 5
zampa-ostras, zampaostras   180
zampullín   off gen— 7-9, applied to smaller grebes
— chico, z. común   off 9
— cuellinegro   off 8
— cuellirrojo   off 7
— orejudo   bkn scl 7
zancas largas, zancolín   238
zancuda   (1) pop sp 238; (2) bkn nonsp/order— 180-245 waders
zancudo común   238
zaramagullón   improp? sp 5, 8? +?
zarapito   (1) pop nonsp? not distinguished? 201, 202; (2) off gen 201-
    204 curlews
— común   202
— de casquete   202
— — pico delgado, z. de pico fino   bkn scl 204
— esquimal   off 203
— fino   off 204
— menor   204
— real   off pop 201
— trinador   off 202
— — común   off 202a

zarapito trinador hudsónico   off scl 202b

[zarcerillo   Guadalajara "pajarito que vive entre zarzales" ?]

zarcero   (1) /?/ 444 +?; (2) off gen 423-427 warblers (−); (3) [Arag "parecido al verderón" ?]

— común   off 424

— escita   off 427

— grande   off 425

— icterino   off scl 423

— pálido   off scl 426

zarceta   var cerceta pop reg 57 or 59

— de invierno   Mex 57

— de otoño, z. de verano   Mex 56

— menor   bkn 57

— tulera   Mex 56

zarzalera   pop nonsp? 460, 462 chats

[zarzalero   Andal =/gagachín/(cagachín)/439?/, /453?/, 460?]

zorzal   (1) pop sp 494; (2) off pop nonsp/gen+ with qualifiers 482-489, 492-495, 497 thrushes; (3) conf? improp sp 489, 493, 495

— carigrís   off 482

— charlo   off 495

— colirrojo   off 484

— común   off 494

— de Naumann   off scl 488b

— dorado   off 497

— eunomo   off scl 488a

— malvís   off 493

— papinegro   off scl 487a

— papirrojo   off scl 487b

— real   off 489

— rojigrís   off 486

— siberiano   off scl 492

— unicolor   off scl 485

— ustulado   off scl 483

zumacaya   var zumaya (1) 45; (2) 314

zumaya   (1) pop nonsp? or not distinguished? 321, 322; (2) arch pop 45; (3) arch pop 314

zura   var zurita 296 [295?]

[zurdal   Palencia = azor 124?]

zurita   pop sp, not distinguished 295, 296

zurriaga   pop Andal 367

APPENDIX

OF NAMES NOT RECORDED IN SPANISH DICTIONARIES

Asterisked*, recorded, but not as a bird-name.
For further explanations see Introduction pp. 26-27.

* abuja
* abujeta
aburraca
agarrapatosa
agateador
aguiloria
* agujeta
alfarfera
alfarfero
alimocha
almendrita
alzacola
ampélido
ampelis
andahuertas
anduriña
* ánima
anserata
* arán
arciucha
arenatela
* arenosa
* aro
ascle
* azulillo
azulón

baquiñuela
barbajelena
* barbón
* barbudo

becacica
becafigos
bernacha
* bigotudo
bilorio
boceta
* bolsicón
bonasa
boñiguero
bubía
bubillo
bubulco
buitrecilla
buitrecillo
* buitrón
bújaro
* bujo
burano
buscarla
* buso
busqueta
buzardo

* cabezón
* cabezota
cagaestacas
caganchina
cágalo
* cagarropa
cagarropas
cajaílla

* cajonera
* calandrina
calcidrán
calidris
camacho
camancho
camara
canastela
* canastera
cangrejerita
canut
cañamera
capiblanco
* capitán
cara de juez
* carambolo
carbonerito
* carniza
* carolo
carpódaco
carrecera
carregadora
carricerín
carricero
* carrión
carrisalero
carrizalero
* cascapiñones
castañita
catabejas
catalinita
cencerrillo

142

* cerillo
cerín
cerrajillo
chamarís
chamarreto
* charrán
charrancito
* chasco
* chata
chepecha
* chilla
* chimbo
chimita
chindor
chirlerona
chirlito
* chirlo
chirriscla
* chirta
* chispita
chochín
chochita
chorlitejo
churlita
churrica
churrilla
churruca
cicí
cierrapuño
* cigüenela, etc.
cinceta
cinguinela
cip, cip-cip
* cistícola
* cite
cité
citrinela
* coletero
coliazul
colirrubio
* coquinero
* corneta
cornichuela
correlimos
correplaya
cotorrito
críalo
cucito

cucua
cujada
cujaílla
culadera
* culebrera
culirrojo
curita

dendroica
* diablo
dormitón

elano
* engañamuchachos
erismaturo
* escribiente
escribiera
escuatarola
* espantadizo
espulgabueyes
esquilaso
estarno
* estercolero
* estercorario
estrellina
estrelliña

falarópodo
* fardela
* friolenco
* frisa
* friso
fulmar
fumarel

* gacha
galdón
galdona
* garcete
garcilla
gargantiazul
gargantirrojo
garrapatera
garrapino

garrapinos
gateador
* gollería
grajilla
grajillo
grébul
grévol
* guerrero

harelda
havelda
* herrero
herreroche

jacaralla
jamas
jaracalla
jarero
jilguerillo
* junco

lililo
liñacero
locustela
lubano
lúbano
lúgano

* malvasía
maquetes
* marismeña
* mataperros
matinero
meleón
mileón
* millero
* mito
* molinero
mondra
monigero
* montañés
morinelo
* mormón
* mosqueta

143

mosquilla
* mosquitera
* mosquitero
muscicapa

* negrón
* nevadilla
* nevera
nictícorax
niotilta
* niso
noveleta
nucifraga

págalo
* pagaza
paino
pajaraco
* paleta
* paleto
* paletón
* palmera
* papavientos
papicolorado
papirrojo
paporrubio
pardote
* parlanchín
* parpar
parula
pastorcilla
* patera
* patiseco
pazpallá
pechel
pechiazul
* pechiblanco
pechirrubio
* pedrero
pegarrebordas
pelarrocas
pelidna
peñasca
peñato
* percha

* perdicero
pernetero
picabuey
picabueyes
picafigos
picanzo
picapinos
picapotros
picapuertas
picatocino
picharchar
picoideo
* picotero
* picotijera
pico-tuerto
* picuda
* pilato
pildoré
pillera
pilotero
* pimpín
pinchahigos
* pinche
pinzoleta
pinzoletica
pinzoletita
* piñata
piornero
piroftalmo
* pisco
pitaciega
* pitillo
pitobarrenos
pitorrelincho
* pitorro
pitrulín
píulo
plectrófano
* pluvial
potorra
* potorro
* potrilla
potrito
primita
pufino
pulverilla
purgabueyes

quebrantón
* quinceta
quivevive

rabiblanca
* rabilarga
rabirrojo
rabitojo
ralo
* ratonero
rebiruelo
* redolín
rejilero
rendaja
reznero
* robín
* roquero
* roseta
rubita
ruhilla
ruiblanca
ruipego

sabubilla
* sacristán
salseno
saltamimbres
* salteador
saradillo
sarceta
* sardinero
sarseruelo
serín
* serpentario
serrata
* serratilla
* serreta
sietearreldes
silvarronco
sita
* sobrestante
soldadito
soldía
soldilla
* solitaria

* sula
surnia
surnio

* tarro
terrerilla
terrerita
terreruela
* tintín
* tintorero
tinúnculo
tordino
torrondana

tótano
totano
treparriscos
trepatorres
* triguero
tringa
triorque
troglodito
tumanavilla

uria
uría

vaqueruela
vencejillo
verdoncillo
* viñera
vuelvepiedras

* zambullidor
zampaostras
zampullín
zancas largas
zancolín
* zancudo
zarzalera
zura

INDEX

OF ENGLISH NAMES

For explanations see Introduction pp. 27-29.

bitterns 46-49
Black-and-white warbler 501
black-backed gull, v. 251, 252
Black-bellied lapwing = Sociable plover 182
Black-bellied plover (Am.) = Grey plover 191
Black-bellied sand-grouse 291
Black-billed cuckoo 305
Blackbird 491
Black brant (Am.) = Brent-goose 100
Black-browed albatross 11
Blackcap 431
Black-capped chickadee (Am.) = Willow-tit 505
Black-capped petrel 29
Blackcock = male Black grouse 151
Black cormorant = Cormorant 33
Black crow = Carrion-crow 399a
Black-crowned night-heron (Am.)=Night-heron 45
Black curlew = Glossy ibis 53
Black eagle = Golden eagle 111
Black-eared wheatear 465
Black-faced bunting 564
Black game (pl.), Black grouse 151
black geese 100-103
Black guillemot 287
Black-headed bunting 562
Black-headed gull 263, v. also 257, 261
Black-headed wagtail 377g
Black-headed warbler = Sardinian warbler 436
Black kite 126
Black lark 361
Black-legged kittiwake (Am.) = Kittiwake 266
Black martin = Swift 325
Black-necked grebe 8
Black oystercatcher 180b
Black redshank = Spotted redshank 213
Black redstart 473
Black scoter = Common scoter 79
Black starling = Spotless starling 389
Black stork 51
Black swift = Plain swift 329
Black-tailed godwit 205
Black tern 267, v. also 268
Black-throated diver 1
Black-throated green warbler 500
Black-throated loon (Am.) = Black-throated diver 1
Black-throated thrush 487a
Black-throated wheatear = Black-eared wheatear 465
Black vulture 109
Black wheatear 468
Black-winged kite 127
Black-winged pratincole 244
Black-winged stilt 238

Black woodpecker 346
Blue-cheeked bee-eater 335
Blue goose = Snow-goose 97
Blue-headed wagtail 377a
Blue rock = Rock-dove 296
Blue rock-thrush 472
Bluethroat 480
Blue tit 510
Blue-winged teal 56
Blyth's reed-warbler 419
Bonaparte's gull 260
Bonaparte's sandpiper 226
Bonelli's eagle 117
Bonelli's warbler, Bonelli's willow-warbler 443
Bonxie = Great skua 247
Booted eagle 118
Booted warbler 427
Bottle-tit = Long-tailed tit 503
Brahminy duck = Ruddy shield-duck 91
Bramble-finch, Brambling 527
Brent-goose 100
Bridled tern 276
Broad-billed sandpiper 234
Brown-backed warbler = Rufous warbler 470
Brown creeper (Am.) = Tree-creeper 517
Brown flycatcher 459
Brown-headed gull = Black-headed gull 263
Brown linnet = Linnet 535
Brown owl = Tawny owl 314
Brünnich's guillemot, Brünnich's murre (Am.) 286
Buff-backed heron = Cattle-egret 44
Buff-breasted sandpiper 235
Buffel-head, Buffel-headed duck, Bufflehead 75
Buffon's skua = Long-tailed skua 249
Bullfinch 545
Bulwer's petrel 26
buntings 547-570
bush-quail, bustard-quail, button-quail, v. 161
bustards 177-179
Buzzard 119
buzzards 119-121

Cabot's tern (Am.) = Sandwich tern 278
Calandra lark 359
Calloo = Long-tailed duck 76
Canada goose 102
Canarian chaffinch 525b
Canarian laurel-pigeon 299
Canarian oystercatcher = Black oystercatcher 180b
Canarian pipit = Berthelot's pipit 370
Canary 530
Canary Islands chaffinch 526

Dunter = Eider 82
Dupont's lark 356
Dusky redshank = Spotted redshank 213
Dusky shearwater = Sooty shearwater 25
Dusky thrush 488a
Dusky warbler 445
dwarf bittern, v. 47
dwarf bitterns 46-47

Eagle-owl 309
eagles 111-118
Eared grebe (Am.) = Black-necked
grebe 8
Eastern grey-lag 92b
Eastern turtle-dove = Rufous turtle-
dove 302
egrets 41-44
Egyptian nightjar 323
Egyptian vulture 107
Eider, Eider-duck 82
eiders 81-84
Eleonora's falcon 142
Erne = White-tailed eagle 128
Eskimo curlew 203
European black-headed gull (Am.) =
Black-headed gull 263
European widgeon (Am.) = Wigeon 63
Eversmann's warbler = Arctic warbler
449
Eye-browed thrush 486

Falcated teal 61
falcons 137-147
Fantail, Fan-tailed warbler 453
Fantail snipe = Snipe 196
Ferruginous duck = White-eyed pochard
72
Fieldfare 489
finches 528-546
Firecrest, Fire-crested wren 452
Fischer's eider (Am.) = Spectacled eider
84
Fish-hawk = Osprey 136
Flamingo 54
Florida gallinule (Am.) = Moorhen 174
flycatchers 454-459
Fork-tailed petrel = Leach's petrel 16
Fox-sparrow 567
Francolin 157
French partridge = Red-legged partridge
156
frigate-birds 36
Frigate-petrel 19
Fuerteventuran chat = Canary Islands
stonechat 461
Fulmar, Fulmar-petrel 31
Furze-wren = Dartford warbler 439

Gadwall 62
gallinules 171-174
Gannet 32
Garden-warbler 430
Garganey 59
geese 92-103
Glaucous gull 255
Glead = Kite 125
Glossy ibis 53
goatsuckers = nightjars 321-324
godwits 205-206
Goldcrest, Gold-crested wren 451
Golden eagle 111
Golden-eye 73, v. also 74
Golden mountain-thrush 497
Golden oriole 386
Golden plover 192, v. also 193
Goldfinch 533
Goosander 88
goose 92-103
Goshawk 124
Gran Canarian blue chaffinch, subsp.
Canary Islands chaffinch 526
Grasshopper-warbler 413, v. also 409, 412
grasshopper-warblers 409-414
Grass-warbler = Fan-tailed warbler 453
Gray sea-eagle (Am.) = White-tailed eagle
128
Gray's grasshopper-warbler 409
Great auk 283
Great black-backed gull = Greater black-
backed gull 251
Great black-headed gull 257
Great black woodpecker = Black wood-
pecker 346
Great bustard 177
Great crested grebe 5
Greater black-backed gull 251
Greater sand-plover 190
Greater scaup (Am.) = Scaup 69
Greater spotted woodpecker 340
Greater whitethroat = Whitethroat 432
Greater yellowlegs, Greater yellowshank
214
Great grey owl 315
Great grey shrike 385
Great northern diver 2
Great reed-warbler 422
Great shearwater 23
Great skua 247
Great snipe 197
Great spotted cuckoo 304
Great spotted woodpecker = Greater
spotted woodpecker 340
Great tit 312
Great white heron = Large egret 42
grebes 5-9
Green-backed gallinule 172
Green cormorant = Shag 34
Greenfinch 531

149

11

Lesser grey shrike 384
Lesser kestrel 145
Lesser purple gallinule = Allen's galli-
nule 173
Lesser redpoll, subsp. Redpoll 536
Lesser short-toed lark 358
Lesser spotted eagle 116
Lesser spotted woodpecker 343
Lesser tern = Little tern 277
Lesser white-fronted goose 94
Lesser whitethroat 433
Lesser yellowlegs 215
Levantine shearwater 20b
Levant sparrow-hawk 123
Light-mantled sooty albatross 14
Linnet 535
Little auk 284
Little bittern 46
Little bunting 557
Little bustard 178
Little crake 168
Little egret 41
Little grebe 9
Little gull 262
Little owl 313
Little ringed plover 186
Little shearwater 21
Little stint 223
Little tern 277
Lobed-footed stint = Grey phalarope 239
Long-eared owl 317
Long-legged petrel = Wilson's petrel 15
Long-legged buzzard 121
Longtail, Long-tail = Long-tailed duck 76
Long-tailed bunting = Siberian meadow-
bunting 551
Long-tailed duck 76
Long-tailed jaeger (Am.), Long-tailed skua
249
Long-tailed tit 503
loons (Am.) = divers 1-4

Macqueen's bustard = Houbara bustard
179
Madagascar bee-eater = Blue-cheeked bee-
eater 335
Madeiran black swift, subsp. Plain swift
329
Madeiran petrel 17
Madeiran pigeon 298
Madeiran quail 159b
Magnificent frigate-bird, Magnificent man-
o'-war bird 36
Magpie 393, v. also 392
Mallard 55
Mandarin, Mandarin duck 67
Manx shearwater 20
Marbled duck, Marbled teal 58
Marmora's warbler 440

Marsh-harrier 131
Marsh-hawk (Am.) = Hen-harrier 132
Marsh-owl = African marsh-owl 319
Marsh-sandpiper 217
Marsh-tit 504
Marsh-warbler 420
Masked bunting = Black-faced bunting
564
Masked shrike 382
Mavis = Song-thrush 494
Meadow-pipit 374
Mealy redpoll, subsp. Redpoll 536
Mediterranean black-headed gull 261
Mediterranean curlew = Slender-billed
curlew 204
Mediterranean falcon 138b
Mediterranean great shearwater =
Mediterranean shearwater 24
Mediterranean gull = Mediterranean
black-headed gull 261
Mediterranean shearwater 24
Melodious warbler 424
Merganser = Red-breasted merganser 87
Merlin 143
Middle spotted woodpecker 344
Missel-thrush, Mistle-thrush 495
Mollymawk = Black-browed albatross 11
Montagu's harrier 134
Moor-buzzard = Marsh-harrier 131
Moorhen 174
Mountain accentor = Siberian accentor
405
Mountain blackbird = Ring-ouzel 490
Mountain-finch = Brambling 527
Mountain-linnet = Twite 534
mountain-thrush, v. 497
Moussier's redstart 475
Moustached swamp-warbler, Moustached
warbler 415
Muriel's chat, subsp. Canary Islands
stonechat 461
murres (Am.) = guillemots 285-287
Mute swan 104

Narcissus flycatcher 456
Naumann's thrush 488b
Needle-tailed swift 330
night-hawk, v. 324
night-hawks (Am.) = nightjars 321-324
Night-heron 45
Nightingale 477
Nightjar 321
nightjars 321-324
Noddy 281
Nordmann's pratincole = Black-winged
pratincole 244
Norfolk plover = Stone-curlew 241
North Atlantic great shearwater, North
Atlantic shearwater 24

Red phalarope (Am.) = Grey phalarope 239
Redpoll 536, v. also 537
Red-rumped swallow 351
Redshank 212, v. also 213
Red-shouldered hawk = Black-winged kite 127
Red-spotted bluethroat 480b
Redstart 474
redstarts 473-475
Red-tailed fieldfare = Naumann's thrush 488b
Red-throated diver, Red-throated loon (Am.) 4
Red-throated pipit 375
Red-throated thrush 487b
Redwing 493
Reed-bunting, Reed-sparrow 565
Reed-warbler, Reed-wren 421, v. also 419, 422
Reeve = female Ruff 236
Richardson's skua = Arctic skua 246
Richard's pipit 368
Ring-dotterel = Ringed plover 185
Ring-dove = Wood-pigeon 297
Ringed plover 185, v. also 186
Ring-necked pheasant (Am.) = Pheasant 160
Ring-ouzel 490
Ring-plover = Ringed plover 185
River-warbler 411
robber-gulls = skuas 246-249
Robin 476
Robin (Am.) = American robin 496
Rock-bunting 550
Rock-dove 296
Rock-nuthatch 515
Rock-partridge 154
Rock-pigeon = Rock-dove 296
Rock-pipit 376b
Rock-ptarmigan (Am.) = Ptarmigan 150
Rock-sparrow 523
Rock-thrush 471
rock-thrushes 471-472
Roller 336
Rook 398
Roseate pelican = White pelican 37
Roseate tern 274
Rose-coloured pastor, Rose-coloured starling 387
Rose-finch = Scarlet grosbeak 539, v. also 540
Ross's gull 264
Rosy pastor = Rose-coloured starling 387
Rough-legged buzzard, Rough-legged hawk (Am.) 120
Royal tern 279
Royston crow = Hooded crow 399b
Ruby-throat 479
Ruddy shell-duck 91

Ruddy turnstone (Am.) = Turnstone 195
Ruff 236
Rufous buzzard = Desert buzzard 119a
Rufous-naped falcon = Barbary falcon 138c
Rufous-naped nightjar = Red-necked nightjar 322
Rufous turtle-dove 302
Rufous warbler 470
Rüppell's warbler 435
Rustic bunting 559

Sabine's gull 265
Saharan blue-cheeked bee-eater, subsp. Blue-cheeked bee-eater 335
Saharan bunting, Saharan house-bunting = Striped bunting 556
Saker falcon 140
Sanderling 233
sand-grouse 291-294
Sand-martin 348
sandpipers 207-235
Sandwich tern 278
Sardinian starling = Spotless starling 389
Sardinian warbler 436
Savi's warbler 410
sawbills 86-89
Scandinavian rock-pipit 376c
Scarlet bullfinch, Scarlet grosbeak 539
Scaup 69
Schlegel's petrel = Kermadec petrel 27
Scops owl 308
scoters 77-79
Screech-owl = Barn-owl 307
Sea-eagle = White-tailed eagle 128
sea-eagles 128-129
sea-gulls 250-266
Sea-magpie = Oystercatcher 180
Sea-parrot = Puffin 290
Sedge-bird, Sedge-warbler 417
Semi-palmated plover (Am.) = Ringed plover 185
Semi-palmated sandpiper 232
Serin, Serin-finch 529
Shag 34
Sharp-tailed sandpiper = Siberian pectoral sandpiper 228
shearwaters 20-25
Sheld-drake = male Sheld-duck 90
Shelduck, Sheld-duck 90, v. also 91
Shore-lark 362
Short-billed gull (Am.) = Common gull 254
Short-eared owl 318
Short-toed eagle 135
Short-toed lark 357, v. also 358
Short-toed tree-creeper 518
Short-winged yellow tree-warbler = Melodious warbler 424

ANALYTIC INDEX OF GLOSSARY PART I

Figures refer to glossary entries, *not* pages.